# Climber's Guide to Devil's Lake

*Preparation of this guide was sponsored by*
*the Chicago Mountaineering Club*

# Climber's Guide
# to Devil's Lake

*Second Edition, Revised and Enlarged*

## Sven Olof Swartling

The University of Wisconsin Press

*A North Coast Book*

The University of Wisconsin Press
114 North Murray Street
Madison, Wisconsin 53715

3 Henrietta Street
London WC2E 8LU, England

Copyright © 1979, 1995
The Board of Regents of the University of Wisconsin System

5   4   3   2   1

Printed in the United States of America

Library of Congress Cataloging-in-Publication Data
Swartling, Sven Olof.
    Climber's guide to Devil's Lake / Sven Olof Swartling.
  — 2nd ed., rev. and enl.
    256 p.          cm.
    Rev. ed. of: Climber's guide to Devil's Lake / William Widule &
Sven Olof Swartling. 1979.
    "A North Coast book."
    Includes bibliographical references (p. 242) and index.
    ISBN 0-299-14594-8
    1. Rock climbing—Wisconsin—Devil's Lake—Guidebooks.
2. Devil's Lake (Wis.)—Guidebooks.   I. Widule, William.
Climber's guide to Devil's Lake.        II. Title.
GV199.42.W62D487          1995
796.5'223'0975576—dc20          94-24116

# Contents

# Illustrations

# Diagrams

## WEST BLUFF

# Warning

Rock climbing is a high-risk sport; your safety and that of your climbing companions is dependent on your experience and judgment in making climbing decisions. This is only a guide-book; it will inform you on the whereabouts and difficulties of known rock-climbing routes. It is not intended to be an instruction book. It is entirely the responsibility of the climber to judge his or her ability to do a route safely. The reader should realize that climbing has potential dangers, and hereby release the author, publisher, and distributors of this book from liability for any injury, including death, that might result.

# Introduction to the
# Second Edition

Since the first printing of this guidebook in 1979, enormous changes have taken place in the rock-climbing scene. The sport has become immensely popular, with a corresponding huge increase in the number of climbers at Devil's Lake and elsewhere. Although the guidebook was reprinted, it has not been revised since the first printing. This edition has a considerable number of changes, additions, and corrections, and has twice the number of climbs in the first edition. Many new routes in all areas have been added, and new areas are described. In addition to all the climbs described in the earlier book, this edition includes climbs in the sandstone area, and climbs east and west of the quarry (it should be noted, however, that climbing in the worked quarry and the sandstone area is presently prohibited).

The evolutionary development of sport climbing is paralleled in the writing of guidebooks for Devil's Lake, and guidebooks have changed considerably since 1965 when the Chicago Mountaineering Club published the first guide to climbs in that area. In the early days of climbing at Devil's Lake, during the 1920s and 1930s, there was little need for a formal guide to the list of available climbs. The small number of climbers had a few favorite climbs, and did a lot of exploring of routes. Information about the climbs was spread by word of mouth, and few records were kept. With the organization of area climbing clubs in 1940, principally the Chicago Mountaineering Club (CMC) and the Iowa Mountaineers, more climbers came to the lake, and the need for reliable and detailed information about climbing routes became necessary. With the ever-increasing numbers of people being attracted to the sport, it became essential to bring to their attention routes that might otherwise be ignored, and thus, it is hoped, spread the climbers over a larger area.

One of the earliest attempts to list climbs at Devil's Lake is a manuscript typed in 1941 titled *Rock Climbing in the Chi-*

*cago Area—An Historic Guide* by Jack Fralick. Unpublished, it lists over 20 routes on the East and West Bluffs, and identifies first ascents by members of the CMC (it's unclear, but unlikely, that unaffiliated climbers made prior first ascents of the difficult routes). Another guide, compiled by William Plumley in 1941, also titled *Rock Climbing in the Chicago Area,* is a set of 8 × 10 photos of climbing at Devil's Lake and elsewhere, and contains annotated material both historical and descriptive in nature.

By the early 1950s, and with a growing organization of climbers, the concept of a comprehensive rock-climbing guide to the entire Devil's Lake area was suggested. From time to time descriptions of climbing routes appeared in the CMC's *Newsletter.* In 1965 the CMC published a preliminary edition of Bill Primak's *Guide to the Practice Climbing Areas of the Chicago Mountaineering Club, Devil's Lake Section.* This guide summarized the club's activities in the early 1950s, and covered the entire climbing area. Routes were described in terms of their problems rather than by a formal classification system. Much attention was given to the older and traditional routes, at the time preferred for their similarity to problems one might encounter in the mountains. Primak was guided by the philosophy in the CMC at the time: namely, that climbing at the lake was not an end in itself, but rather a training ground for climbing to be done in the mountains. In 1970 the Wisconsin Hoofers published *Climbers and Hikers Guide to Devil's Lake* by David Smith, Roger Zimmerman, and Errol Morris, an exhaustive description of the popular climbing area on the East Bluff above the old Civilian Conservation Corps camp. Unfortunately, only a few other East Bluff climbs and areas are described. The book is a fine example of the prevailing guidebook writing of the period.

In 1979, when the first edition of the present book was published, it described most of the known climbs at that time and contained much information from the previous publications. In addition to diagramming and describing most of the climbs known then, the book provided the usual fare of natural history information, as well as a hiking trail guide. The book had some shortcomings, a principal objection being the closed NCCS 'F' grading system. The most recent (1985) Devil's Lake guide is Leo Hermacinski's *Extremist's Guide to Devil's Lake New Climbs.* This small guidebook is a listing of several routes put up since the publication of the CMC guidebook. It does not embrace the entire lake area, but concentrates on the East Bluff and Sandstone Area. Most of the new climbs listed are in the range of 5.8 to 5.12 (see p. 36 below). A revised edition of *Extremist's Guide* has been prepared, but Leo has no plans for publication. Both of his guides include historic information on first ascents, first leads, and other commentary.

This revised edition of *Climber's Guide to Devil's Lake* has been long in preparation and is the definitive guide to the entire region. It is the product of the effort of many individuals, and by permission, incorporates information from previous guides. Additionally, it has rectified past errors of omission and commission, and will, we hope, appease the critics of the previous edition.

> George Pokorny
> General Editor, Chicago Mountaineering Club
> *Glen Ellyn, Illinois*
> *February 1994*

# Preface

Devil's Lake, in south-central Wisconsin near Baraboo, provides extraordinary climbing opportunities for the rock climber, sport climber, and mountaineer. The hard quartzite cliffs are a geologic anomaly in a region better known for its unusual sandstone formations. The rock terrain is hard, with sharp fractures, cracks, ledges, slabs, chimneys, and a variety of rock forms that make this the best rock-climbing area in the Midwest. Historically, Devil's Lake has provided enjoyment for hikers and walkers since the mid-1800s, and, doubtless, scrambling over the boulderfields and lower cliffs was also popular. It was not until 1927, however, that true alpine-style rock climbing was introduced to Devil's Lake by Joe and Paul Stettner. Using the traditional climbing techniques of their native Bavarian mountains, the brothers trained countless numbers of midwesterners to the then unique sport of roped rock climbing.

In 1940 the Chicago Mountaineering Club was established, and the lake bluffs became the pre-eminent training area for the club's members. With scheduled monthly climbing weekends at Devil's Lake, they trained additional midwesterners in the sport and prepared them for climbing in the mountains. The decade of the 1960s was marked by continuous raising of the standards, accomplished mostly by college students. John Gill made some exceedingly difficult climbs in 1960–1961, and it was three to four years before anyone else approaching his skill came along. Between 1960 and 1966 some fine routes were developed by climbers from the University of Chicago, with the best routes put up by Richard Goldstone and Steve Derenzo. In 1965–1968 the Wisconsin Hoofers (University of Wisconsin outing club) pushed up several difficult routes on the East Ramparts, which had not been previously climbed. Some of the climbers of that period were Dave and Jim Erickson, Sheldon Smith, Scott Stewart, Errol Morris, and Pete Cleveland. In more recent years the popularity of rock climbing has brought enormous numbers of climbers to the lake, from climbers' clubs and sport gyms with climbing walls, as well as unaffiliated individuals. The list of exceptional people climbing at the upper levels is large, and growing, and since the 1980s the standard of climbing is well beyond what had previously been achieved. Pete Cleveland remains one of the finest climbers at the lake, and others such as Eric Zschiesche, with his ascent of Rubber Man (5.13b) and solo of The Zipper (B2), and Dave Groth, with his ascent of Ice (5.13a), reflect the current high standard of lake ascents. Some other high profile climbers are Tommy Deuchler (first lead on Bagatelle), Ralph Schmitt, Rich Bechler, and Steve Sangdahl.

Devil's Lake State Park continues to suffer from overcrowding; in addition to rock climbers, each year brings more hikers to the trails. It is hoped that this guidebook will help to distribute climbers to areas of the lake that have been overlooked and underclimbed in the past. Many individuals drawn to Devil's Lake were introduced to climbing in physical education classes, in sporting clubs with climbing walls, and by private instruction at Devil's Lake and elsewhere. The newcomers trained on climbing walls find that outdoor climbing at Devil's Lake differs from climbing on an indoor wall. Even talented indoor climbers soon discover that climbing outdoors in the elements can be profoundly different. The natural hand- and footholds are not always obvious, and friction at Devil's Lake, unlike that on an artificial wall, is minimal, to say the least. This is not meant to detract from the beauty of climbing at the lake; it is a unique and satisfying experience.

I hope that the descriptions and grading of the climbs will enable climbers to select climbs that match their skill and ability, and permit them to climb safely. Every effort has been made to include as many climbs as possible and grade them correctly in this guide. There are still routes waiting to be discovered, and I would be grateful if those who make discoveries, or find errors, would contact me or communicate with the Chicago Mountaineering Club.

Sven Olof "Olle" Swartling
*Chicago, Illinois*
*February 1994*

# Acknowledgments

This guidebook contains information contained in the 1979 edition, and new information contained in other guidebooks, routes discovered by myself and others, and the contributions, comments, and ideas of many individuals. The previous edition of this guide was co-authored by Bill Widule. I'm grateful to him for his assistance in building a foundation for this edition.

I would like to thank all the climbers who climbed, and re-climbed, new routes to help determine the proper grade. These unsung heroes are too numerous to mention. I am especially appreciative of the effort of Alex Andrews, for expanding the base of knowledge by initiating and maintaining contact with climbers at Devil's Lake beyond my sphere of contact, and for his comments and information on routes, ratings, etc. Additionally, Alex spent countless hours in front of his computer converting diagrams from paper to electronic representations for this edition. Ralph Schmitt and Saul Sepsenwol deserve special thanks for their input on new climbing routes and ratings. I'm also grateful to the following: Rich Bechler, Pete Cleveland, Bill Dietrich, Dave Groth, Leo Hermacinski, and John Putnam. Without their assistance this guide would not have been possible. Special thanks go to Jim Yarnold for his support in assisting with computer expertise, and to Tony Suszko and Carolyn Griffin for their artwork.

Finally, I want to especially thank my wife Sue who assisted me throughout this process by accompanying me on my explorations, translating my notes into typed copy, and typing the final manuscript.

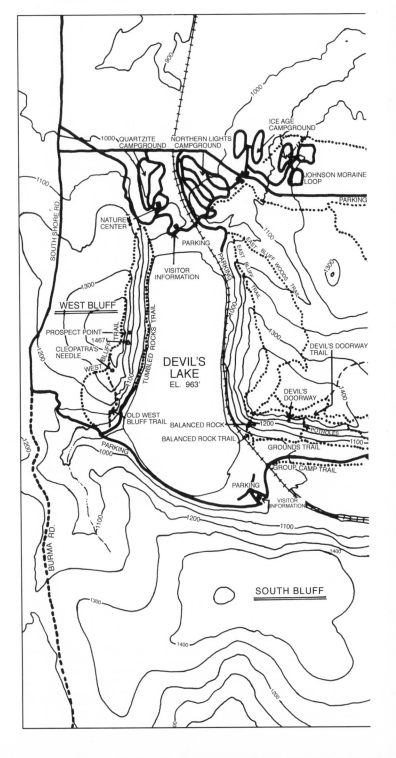

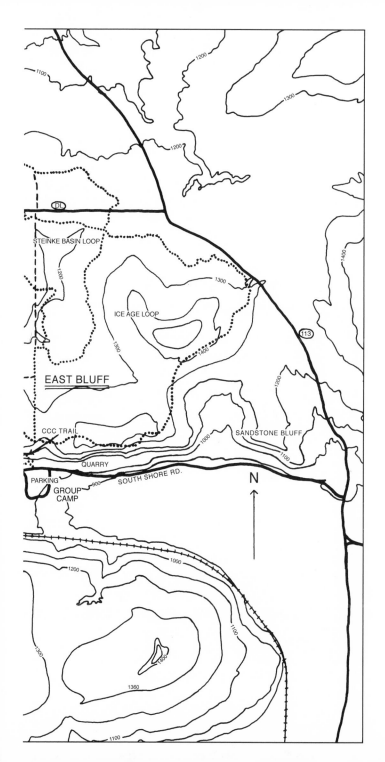

# A Geologic and Natural History of the Baraboo Hills, Wisconsin

## PATRICIA K. ARMSTRONG

Devil's Lake, Wisconsin, is one of the most beautiful and unusual areas in the Midwest. Precambrian seas formed the rock of the Baraboo Range, while Pleistocene glaciers shaped the topography and created the lake and its botanical environment. Devil's Lake itself (approximately 1 mile long and .6 mile wide) lies in a north-south gap cut by preglacial rivers through 500-foot-high bluffs. Cliffs and talus border the lake on three sides. The old river valley trends eastward away from the lake at its south end. Terminal moraines from the last glaciation block the valley east and north of the lake.

## The Formation of the Baraboo Quartzite

The story of the Baraboo quartzite began 1.5 billion years ago in the Huronian period of the Precambrian era beneath a quiet sea. Incredible amounts of nearly pure quartz sand were deposited and accumulated at the bottom of this sea until the weight began to press the sediments together into sandstone. Iron oxide and silica (quartz, $SiO_2$) in solution filled in the spaces and cemented the sand grains together. The pink, red, or purple color resulted from the incorporation of small amounts of iron and manganese. The original formation is thought to have been several miles thick, but weathering throughout the ages has reduced it to its present 4,000–5,000 feet.

Although most quartzite comes from sandstone that has been heated and pressed to fuse the sand grains together, microscopic study of the structure of the Baraboo quartzite reveals that it solidified slowly, without crystal distortion or high-temperature mineral growth. This means that it is essentially sedimentary instead of metamorphic quartzite. Structures such as ripple marks, bedding planes, cross-current stratification, and pebble layers are perfectly preserved. Ripple marks are especially plentiful around Turk's Head on the West Bluff, and pebble layers can be found east of Devil's Doorway on the East Bluff. Areas in the original sea containing silt were lithified into phyllite, which can be seen as thin, slatey rock, sandwiched between quartzite along the CCC Trail to The Guillotine.

Sandstone is dull and porous and breaks around its cemented sand grains, making rounded holds and sandy ledges. Quartzite, although identical to sandstone in chemical composition, is much harder and breaks across its cemented sand grains, producing a smooth, shiny surface and sharp edges. Thus the cliffs at Devil's Lake are much better for climbing than the sandstone cliffs southeast at Gibraltar Rock. On the wall north of Leaning Tower and the cliffs to the east, the cement between the sand grains has weathered away, leaving the rock more like sandstone than quartzite, with slightly different climbing conditions.

## The Building of the Baraboo Range

About 1.45 billion years ago tectonic forces bent, cracked, and folded the huge thickness of Baraboo quartzite into a mountain chain which took the shape of an oval celery dish 10 miles wide and 25 miles long. It trends west-southwest from Interstate 90–94 to a few miles west of Rock Springs, with the village of Baraboo approximately in the middle. The north rim is lower in elevation, with nearly vertical bedding planes visible at the Upper and Lower Narrows of the Baraboo River. The south rim, in which Devil's Lake lies, is higher in elevation and slopes north at 20 to 25 degrees. This can be seen when looking across the lake at either the East or the West Bluffs.

The quartzite was extremely brittle and fractured as it was bent, causing both horizontal and vertical cracks. Some slippage along these cracks occurred, as evidence by pearl-like surfaces on the quartzite. Good examples of polished surfaces are at The Flatiron and a slanted rock in the Balanced Rock Trail that is now almost entirely covered by a flat rock and concrete. Some of the smaller cracks were subsequently filled in by silica solution and show today as white, quartz-filled veins. A few wider ones have angular pieces of quartzite (breccia) mixed with the quartz. Examples are visible along the Potholes Trail on the East Bluff.

## Tropical Islands in the Cambrian Sea

The next geological event is one of the most interesting. About 600 million years ago, the Baraboo Range, having undergone weathering for nearly a billion years, was submerged in a Cambrian sea. At this time, the quartzite mountain roots (called monadnocks) stood 200 to 600 feet above the water as a tropical atoll. A white-to-tan sand mixed with quartzite blocks, boulders, and gravel eroded from the land and was deposited about these islands.

Studies of the orientation of cross stratifications in the sandstone and in boulder/gravel accumulations around the islands, supported by paleomagnetic evidence, has led some scientists to postulate that the lagoon and atoll were located in a trade wind zone 10 degrees south of the Cambrian equator.

Fine examples of the cross-bedded Cambrian sandstone with quartzite boulders and gravel can be seen up the Koshawago Spring Valley (southwest of the lake) and at Parfrey's Glen (5 miles east of the lake). Near the north end of the East Bluff, in the vicinity of Elephant Cave, are other examples of conglomerate and sandstone formations. Elephant Rock itself bears evidence of wave polishing received when it rested on the shores of the Cambrian sea.

## The Missing Record and Mysterious Rivers

Other sandstones, limestones, and dolomites were deposited around the quartzite islands until the Ordovician period some 430 million years ago. These can be seen at Gibraltar Rock and other places south and west of the Baraboo Range. From then until the advance of the Pleistocene glaciers one million years ago little is known. If other deposits were laid down, they have since been removed and nothing can be learned about them.

Sometime before the first advance of the glaciers, tremendous rivers cut through the quartzite, making the gaps now filled by the Baraboo River (Upper and Lower Narrows) and Devil's Lake itself. A well drilled at the south shore in 1990 apparently hit bedrock at 419 feet, making the old river channel where Devil's Lake lies approximately 1,000 feet below the present bluff tops.

Water-polished gravels called the Windrow Formation, believed to be Cretaceous (150 million years old), have been found above 1,460 feet in elevation on the bluffs. These can be seen near the top of the Potholes Trail on the East Bluff. The potholes themselves are an enigma. They had to be formed at the base of a waterfall, yet they now stand near the top of the bluff. There are also huge boulders bearing potholes in the woods on top of the East Bluff.

## The Pleistocene Glaciers

Several times between a million years ago and the present, glaciers advanced and retreated over the face of the Midwest. In a majority of cases the most recent stage, called the Woodfordian or Cary stage (13,000–16,000 years ago), blotted out all indications of preceding glaciation. The terminal moraine from this glacier averages 20 to 60 feet high and 300 feet wide. It snakes its way across Wisconsin and covers half of the Baraboo Range. Portions of this terminal moraine are seen as prominent forest-covered ridges at the north end of Devil's Lake and across the valley east of the south end of the lake. Devil's Lake lies between them, just outside the glaciated area.

Scientists long ago recognized a narrow island of topography in northwestern Illinois, southwestern Wisconsin, northeastern Iowa, and southeastern Minnesota as being very different from the rest of the Midwest. It was long thought to be nonglaciated and was called the Driftless Area. Today some scientists think that the Driftless Area was glaciated by earlier, slow-moving glaciers that left little evidence of their passing. Small, round kettle-ponds west of Baraboo, mixed gravel and sand, till-like deposits near Leland, and large boulders out of place, like the pothole rocks on top of the East Bluff, may indicate that glaciers were in the Driftless Area before the Woodfordian era.

In any case, from 12,500 to 30,000 years ago the climate

around Devil's Lake was like that in the high Arctic today. Temperatures dropped below freezing several times during the day and night. Water trapped in the cracks and joint planes of the quartzite repeatedly froze and thawed. This frost plucking/ice wedging caused huge blocks to topple from the cliffs, making the talus below. Cleopatra's Needle, Turk's Head, Tomahawk Rock, Balanced Rock, and Devil's Doorway were produced in this manner.

The last glacier advanced over the Baraboo Hills about 13,000 years ago and stood stationary around Devil's Lake for 600 years. It filled in the ancient river valley with two billion cubic feet of debris. Some of it slumped down into the pre-existing boulderfields to form the cool depressions along the Grottos Trail. Runoff from the melting ice brought the sand for the swimming beaches and filled the gap between the bluffs and moraines with the waters of Devil's Lake.

Finally the glaciers disappeared and the ancient river (which used to run through the Lower Narrows and Devil's Lake Gap) was diverted elsewhere. Devil's Lake today is several hundred feet above the Wisconsin River. It is 45 feet deep, is fed by springs and two small creeks, and has no surface outlet. The water is clean and cold and is lost by seepage and evaporation. The lake's beautiful setting, surrounded by pink cliffs and boulderfields, provides many habitats for plants and animals, as well as an attractive place for outdoor sports of all kinds.

## Plants and Animals

The uniqueness of the Devil's Lake area owes much to its geologic past. Without the quartzite bluffs and boulderfields, glacial lakes, outwash plains, and moraines there would be less varied habitats for plant and animal life. The area not covered by the most recent glaciation acted as a *refugium* where plants and animals could live while the rest of the area was under ice. These relic communities from the past spread out and met other plant communities reinvading the newly bared glacial landscape from the north and south. About 900 species of vascular plants grow in the park, approximately 40 percent of all the species of vascular plants in the whole state.

On top of the bluffs are upland forests, composed primarily

of oaks with an understory of red maple. There are also a few hickories and basswoods. On dry southern exposures juniper and rare plants from the south (like prickly pear cactus) can be found. Hill or goat prairies have tall prairie grasses, creamy baptisia, lead-plant, bush clover, shooting star, yellow star grass, bird-foot violet, and other plants typical of the grasslands to the south and west of Wisconsin.

The cliffs and boulderfields are home to white pine, paper birch, mountain ash, Virginia creeper and poison ivy vines, red elderberry, alum root, pale corydalis, cup plant, many species of ferns, and hundreds of different mosses and lichens. Narrow glens and canyons hold the most exotic plants, such as hemlocks, yellow birch, blue beech, twisted-stalk, Canada May flower, dwarf ginseng, trailing arbutus, and shining club moss. Cold grottos at the base of the boulderfield have rare northern plants like mountain maple, beaked hazel, shin leaf, oak fern, palm tree, moss, and rose moss. Nearby lowlands have kettle ponds, wet meadows, sand prairies, and tamarack-sphagnum bogs.

Because of the rich assortment of habitats and plants, there are a great number of animals too. Approximately 110 species of birds nest here, and more than a hundred additional species can be seen in migration. The rare peregrine falcon used to nest at the lake. Of particular interest are turkey vultures, pileated woodpeckers, whippoorwills, and winter wrens. Occasionally, bald eagles and ospreys fly over the bluffs.

The largest mammal in Devil's Lake State Park is the white-tailed deer. Gray and red foxes also occur, but are rarely seen. Many small mammals, such as raccoons, woodchucks, squirrels, and chipmunks, are common visitors to the campgrounds. There are 30 kinds of mammals altogether.

Ten species of snakes occur, including the beautiful yellow phase of the timber rattlesnake. This snake is not common, however, and is very secretive and rarely seen. There are also eight types of frogs, one toad, four types of turtles, and five types of salamanders. In the lake itself are northerns, walleyes, rainbow and brown trout, small and large mouth bass, perch, and several types of panfish.

Vulnerable areas where rare and unusual plants or animals live need to be protected from trampling and overuse. Most people do not recognize rare plants, and indiscriminate hiking and snowmobiling, cutting firewood, and vandalizing rocks have been very harmful. Efforts should be made to restrict human activities in areas of special scientific interest (like Parfrey's Glen, the Grottos, and the South Bluff). Only in this way can their unique flora, fauna, and geologic attractions be saved for future generations to enjoy.

## Man and the Baraboo Hills

At the time that the last glacier was melting from the Baraboo Hills, Paleo Indians were using rock shelters west of the lake. Five hundred generations of Native Americans knew Devil's Lake before the coming of European man. The effigy mound builders built their bird, lynx, and bear mounds around the lake about 600 to 1,200 years ago. In more recent times several Indian tribes, notably the Winnebago, gave their names and interpretations to the lake.

The Winnebago camped at the lake until 1900 and described the forces which shaped it as a battle between thunderbirds and water spirits. Another legend tells of a great meteorite that produced the Devil's Lake Gap and cliffs. The Winnebago name for the lake was "Ta-wa-cun-chuk-dah" or "Da-wa-kah-char-gra," meaning "Sacred Lake," "Holy Lake," or "Spirit Lake." Other Indians called it "Minni-wau-kan," meaning "Bad Spirit Lake" or "Mystery Lake." Mysterious musical hammering sounds were supposedly the source of the intrigue.

While doing research on the lichens and mosses of Devil's Lake, I noticed that when the early morning sun warmed the boulderfields, or when the evening shadows crept across the rocks, strange melodious "plonks" occurred on the average of one to two per minute in one small area. These heat expansion–cool contraction sounds, when heard across the distance of the lake and supported by echoes and sounds from other areas, could be the reason for the Indian name.

French voyageurs and missionaries came south from the Great Lakes and north from the Fox River Valley in the 1630s. Settlers began to arrive in the 1830s. Because of the sandiness of the glacial outwash in this area and the rockiness of the Baraboo Range, much of the land was unsuited for farming and thus remained somewhat wild throughout the years.

The popularity of Devil's Lake as a vacation retreat dates to the mid-1800s. From 1866 to the early 1900s the Minniwauken House (later Cliff House) served thousands of tourists at the north end of the lake. After the railroad was completed in 1873, up to 18 passenger trains a day went by the lake, nine each way. Side-wheel steamers plied the waters. Kirkland, at the south end of the lake, had more rustic cabins and picnic grounds for the public.

Quarrying operations and proliferating resorts led many local people to seek state park status for Devil's Lake. After a long battle the lake became Wisconsin's third state park in 1911. The original purchase was $128,000 for 1,100 acres. (In 1919 the quarry operations were finally removed from the park.)

During the 1930s a Civilian Conservation Corps camp was built a mile east of the lake at the south end. It consisted of 15 buildings and had its own water and sewage systems. Two hundred young men (aged 18–25) arrived at the camp in 1935 and did various jobs throughout the area. They built trails, signs, picnic tables, buildings, and roads. They removed dangerous or infectious plants. They learned about the plants and the park and conducted tours on the bluffs. The CCC program ended in 1941, but the camp served to house employees of a nearby ammunition plant from 1942 to 1945. All the buildings are gone now.

Today Devil's Lake State Park's 9,000 acres hosts over a million visitors a year. An active naturalist program of hikes and slide shows helps them understand the natural history of the park and the necessity of protecting it from the pressures of tourism. In 1971 the park became part of the Ice Age National Scientific Reserve. Users of the Midwest's most popular park must be willing to sacrifice their own selfish comforts for the preservation of this unique and beautiful area.

# Hiking Trails at Devil's Lake

## PATRICIA K. ARMSTRONG

Hiking trails of dirt, gravel, or asphalt have been developed by the CCC men and Devil's Lake Park personnel over the years. Since Devil's Lake has become part of the Ice Age National Scientific Reserve, federal funds will help develop more trails. The interpretation program at the lake includes a Nature Center and museum at the north shore and many trails around the lake and bluffs. Park naturalists give slide programs and lead nature hikes. There are also several self-guided nature trails with booklets that may be picked up at the Nature Center.

Some of the park trails are access trails to the climbing areas. Most are for hikers looking for good exercise and fine views. There is a trail into Parfrey's Glen (5 miles east of the lake). Because of the fragile nature of the rare plant communities, hikers are advised to stay on foot trails or county roads and not walk cross country.

Since most of the climbing is accessible from the south shore of Devil's Lake, hiking trails will be discussed beginning from that end of the lake; they have been divided into geographical areas for ease in locating them on the map.

## The East Bluff

This is the largest bluff, having a north-south trending section along the east side of the lake and an east-west trending section along the north side of the old river valley. Existing trails on the East Bluff include the following:

*East Bluff Trail (1.3 miles)*  This trail is on top of the East Bluff and leads from the south end (Balanced Rock Trail) to the north end of the lake. It offers many fine views of Baraboo to the north, the lake below, and the West Bluff. Tomahawk Rock, Elephant Cave, and Elephant Rock are landmarks along this trail.

*East Bluff Woods Trail (1.3 miles)*　This trail follows the top of the East Bluff from the south to the north end of the lake. It begins and ends in the same area as the East Bluff Trail, but is back in the woods away from the edge of the bluff.

*Devil's Doorway Trail (.5 mile)*　This trail follows the rim of the East Bluff from the lake (Balanced Rock Trail) eastward along the valley. It offers views of the lake and South Bluff as well as Devil's Doorway and some potholes. From the eastern part of this trail one can see the moraine below and Lake Wisconsin to the southeast.

*Grottos Trail (.7 mile)*　This trail runs along the bottom of the East Bluff in the valley. It offers a cool walk through the woods where large depressions called "grottos" occur. There are many nice views of the talus and cliffs above on the East Bluff.

*Balanced Rock Trail (.3 mile)*　This trail begins at the southeast end of the lake, near the railroad tracks, and climbs the talus to the bluff top, where the East Bluff Trail, East Bluff Woods Trail, and Devil's Doorway Trail meet. The Balanced Rock is about two-thirds of the way up the talus. On top of the bluff, park personnel have encouraged the growth of prairie plants. This trail offers good views of the lake and the South and West Bluffs.

*Potholes Trail (.3 mile)*　This trail connects the Grottos Trail and the Devil's Doorway Trail. It climbs the talus slope, passes through a cleft in the rocks called Red Rocks, and ends up along many fine potholes worn by a prehistoric waterfall.

*CCC Trail (.6 mile)*　This trail climbs the East Bluff above the CCC parking area and turns west along the rim to join the Devil's Doorway Trail. It passes near The Flatiron, The Guillotine, and Leaning Tower and offers fine views of the South Bluff, valley, and Wisconsin River (Lake Wisconsin).

*Trail to Group Camp (.4 mile)*    This trail parallels the road and leads eastward from the south shore picnic area to the Group Camp located near the start of the CCC Trail. It goes through the woods, with some views of the East Bluff above the trees.

## The West Bluff

*West Bluff Trail (1.5 miles)*    This asphalt-covered trail starts on the southwest side of the lake at the junction of South Shore Road and the cottage access road and ascends through the woods to the top of the bluff. It follows the rim of the West Bluff and then descends to the north end of the lake. It offers spectacular views of the lake, the Baraboo Valley to the north, the pre-glacial Wisconsin River valley and Pleistocene glacial moraine to the east, and the Wisconsin River to the southeast. Cleopatra's Needle, Turk's Head, and Prospect Point are landmarks along the way.

*Tumbled Rocks Trail (.8 mile)*    This is also an asphalt trail. It runs along the bottom of the West Bluff between the south and north lake shores, following the west side of the lake through large talus boulders and offering views across the lake to the East Bluff and up the boulderfields to the West Bluff.

Access to climbing areas on the West Bluff are via the Tumbled Rocks Trail and old short-cut trails to the West Bluff Trail.

## The South Bluff

There are no existing trails in this area. There is only one small climbing area on this bluff and no established access trails.

## The Steinke Basin

*Steinke Basin Loop (2.5 miles)*    This grassy and fairly level trail runs through an extinct glacial lake bed.

*Ice Age Loop (4 miles)*  This fairly long trail starts in Steinke Basin, winds through grassy, open fields and woods, reaching the top of the East Bluff near its south end. Here it offers some scenic views of the valley below and Lake Wisconsin.

*Johnson Moraine Loop (2.5 miles)*  This trail runs mostly on the north side of County Highway DL. There are a number of kettle ponds and marshes along the trail.

*Ice Age Trail (4 miles)*  This trail is part of the 1,000-mile Wisconsin Ice Age trail. It runs between the Ice Age Loop trail and Parfrey's Glen.

## The South Shore

*Landmark Nature Trail*  A self-guided trail that starts at the Ranger Station on the south shore and follows landmarks around the picnic area and Grottos Trail to show visitors much of the early history of Devil's Lake State Park. A trail booklet to help the hiker find his way and to explain what he is seeing can be picked up at the Nature Center on the north shore.

## The North Shore

*Indian Mounds Trail*  A self-guided trail which begins at the Nature Center and ends at the north end of the east bluff.

Devil's Lake State Park presently contains about 20 miles of hiking trails. Many of these trails are used for crosscountry skiing as well as hiking.

# Guidebook User's Information

This guidebook locates and describes rock climbs in the Devil's Lake area. The first part, the East Bluff, describes climbs on the east side of Devil's Lake, beginning with the Sandstone Area at the far eastern end of the bluff, near Highway 113. The descriptions proceed westward along the cliffs to Balanced Rock, then to the north shore. The second part describes climbs on the west side of the lake, beginning with Stettner Rocks at the south end of the lake and proceeding northward along the cliff that constitutes the West Bluff.

The bluffs are subdivided into climbing areas, with each area description preceded by a single line contour diagram of that section. Consecutive numbers denote the location of described climbs. *In congested areas, several climbs may be listed under the same number.*

Shaded portions of the contour indicate the area is above other parts of the drawing. Also included on the diagram are a directional arrow indicating compass north (magnetic north), a distance scale in feet, and access trails. Further orientation may be obtained by referring to the map of Devil's Lake.

During the early climbing years at Devil's Lake many first ascents which occurred were not recorded. Because of this great uncertainty regarding the real first ascent, descriptions omit mention of the first ascent or first lead of a route.

## Examples of Ratings

The following climbs are generally taken to be indicative of their class and are frequently used as benchmarks for rating other climbs.

Although all attempts were made to be as uniform as possible in assigning ratings, differences in individual build, technique, and preference make some climbs seem harder or easier than their ratings.

| 1 | The CCC Trail | 5.10a | Congratulations |
| 2 & 3 | East Bluff's talus slope | 5.10b | Cheatah |
| 4 | Lost Face access gully | 5.10c | Jack the Ripper |
| 5.0 | Easy Street | 5.10d | Flake Route |
| 5.1 | The Little Thing | 5.11a | Black Rib |
| 5.2 | Anemia | 5.11b | Callipigeanous Direct |
| 5.3 | Boyscout | 5.11c | Hourglass |
| 5.4 | Beginner's Delight | 5.11d | No Trump |
| 5.5 | The Bone | 5.12a | Double Clutch |
| 5.6 | Brinton's Crack | 5.12b | New Light Waves |
| 5.7 | Vacillation | 5.12c | Steak Sauce |
| 5.8 | Roger's Roof | 5.12d | Phlogiston |
| 5.9 | Upper Diagonal | 5.13a | Ice |
| 5.9+ | Chiaroscuro | 5.13b | Rubber Man |

# Classification of Climbs

The Yosemite Decimal System (YDS) with a " + " added within grade 5.9 is used throughout the guidebook. Following is a comparison of rating systems.

| YDS | modified NCCS* | British | French | German |
|-----|------|---------|--------|--------|
| 1 | F1 | | | |
| 2 | F2 | | | |
| 3 | F2 | | | |
| 4 | F3 | | | |
| 5.0 | F4 | | | |
| 5.1 | F4 | | | |
| 5.2 | F4 | 3a | | |
| 5.3 | F5 | 3b | | |
| 5.4 | F5 | 3c | | |
| 5.5 | F5 | 4d | | |
| 5.6 | F6 | 4b | | |
| 5.7 | F7 | 4c | 5a | 5+ |
| 5.8 | F8 | 5a | 5b | 6− |
| 5.9 | F9A | 5b | 5c | 6 |

| YDS | modified NCCS* | British | French | German |
|------|------|------|------|------|
| 5.9+ | F9B | 5b | 5c | 6+ |
| 5.10a | F9C | 5c | 6a | 6+ |
| 5.10b | F10A | 5c | 6a+ | 7− |
| 5.10c | F10A | 5c | 6b | 7 |
| 5.10d | F10A | 5c | 6b+ | 7+ |
| 5.11a | F10A | 6a | 6c | 7+ |
| 5.11b | F10B | 6a | 6c | 8− |
| 5.11c | F10B | 6a | 6c+ | 8 |
| 5.11d | F10B | 6b | 7a | 8+ |
| 5.12a | F10C | 6b | 7a+ | 9− |
| 5.12b | F10C | 6b | 7b | 9 |
| 5.12c | F10C | 6c | 7b+ | 9 |
| 5.12d | F10C | 6c | 7c | 9+ |
| 5.13a | | 6c | 7c+ | 10− |
| 5.13b | | | 8a | 10 |

*The modified National Climbing Classification System was used in the first edition of the guidebook.

In addition, B1, B2, and B3 are used to rate a few short climbs or "boulder problems."

## Climbing Ethics

More than any other sporting activity, rock climbing needs an ethical code with respect to the environment. Unlike most other forms of recreation, the very essence of rock climbing depends on the natural scene, a nonrenewable resource. The popularity of rock climbing is causing a tremendous human impact upon the cliffs and the surrounding land at Devil's Lake.

The future of climbing is dependent on a minimum-impact approach. The ecological systems have only a brief growing season between melting of the last snows and the onset of long harsh winters. Furthermore, the rock formations broken by the deliberate or thoughtless action of unmindful climbers cannot mend themselves or recover. They are a rather fragile, easily marred, and nonhealing climbing medium. Federal and state agencies, as well as private owners, are increasingly concerned about the protection of this environment. In some areas limitations on use have been imposed. Continuous access to the rock walls at Devil's Lake and elsewhere will depend upon the care with which they are treated.

Therefore, climbers are urged to consider the cumulative effects of climbing activities and follow a code of ethics that will preserve rock-climbing areas and leave them accessible to future generations. Self-restraint and discretion must be employed by every individual in order to preserve the climbing areas and the sport. It is difficult to suggest a set of rules or principles to govern the conduct of people who love freedom and who climb because it makes them feel free. Inasmuch as no specific code of rock-climbing ethics exists, it is recommended that the guidelines given here be followed as a minimum approach to good environmental conduct.

1. *Climb Clean*.  DO NOT USE PROTECTION DEVICES SUCH AS PITONS AND BOLTS. These will permanently deface the rock and degrade the route for subsequent climbers. Nuts and mechanical camming devices have replaced pitons at Devil's Lake, because in addition to affording adequate protection, they leave the rock intact. On a few routes an occasional "fixed" piton may be encountered. These pitons were left in place to protect the rock and should not be removed.

2. *Use Chalk Sparingly If at All*.  Like other climbing aids, the use of chalk is controversial. The usual argument is that it leaves the cliffs unsightly, spoiling the beauty and visual impact. Second, it marks holds for the next climber, spoiling the climb for others. Finally, heavy use of chalk is a form of pollution which rains may not wash away for some period of time. If chalk must be used, it should be used sparsely and only on the most severe pitches.

3. *Protect the Flora*.  The area beneath a climbing line, or a belay stance above the climbing line, is frequently off the trail and may be near flowers or a grassy patch. If the climbing party is large, the impact of many climbing boots may be too much for the delicate micro-environment to bear. This situation is difficult to resolve. If at all possible, try to refrain from overuse of such areas, or stay on the rocks near the start of the climb while awaiting your turn to climb. Also, when hiking or approaching a climb, climbers should stay on the trail as much as possible

to minimize the abuse of delicate plant life. Another abuse perpetrated by climbers is the "gardening" of ledges or holds, frequently removing entire plant colonies from the cliff face. This practice is difficult to defend. It is hoped that awareness of the problem will lead to a certain amount of restraint.

4. *Protect the Trees.* Continuous use for belay and rappel anchors can damage and even kill trees.

5. *Don't Litter.* Climbers who carry food and beverages with them should carry all resulting trash and garbage back to suitable trash containers. Additionally, the concerned climber will pack out litter left behind by the thoughtless person who will always be with us, no matter how high the general level of consciousness becomes.

6. *Be Considerate of Fellow Climbers.* Respect for other climbers should be expressed in a sportsmanlike manner. Don't hog climbs. It is very inconsiderate to drop several ropes on nearby climbs and then climb one route at a time. This may "reserve" climbs for your party, but it prevents others from climbing in the same area. As Devil's Lake becomes more crowded, climbers must learn to share the limited routes with others.

7. *Observe Devil's Lake Regulations.* The climbing areas described in this guidebook are entirely within Devil's Lake State Park. Therefore, climbers should be familiar with park regulations as outlined in the Visitor's Guide available at Park Headquarters. Park users have a responsibility to become familiar with these regulations and abide by them.

## Safety

Your enjoyment of climbing at Devil's Lake will be greater if a few simple safety rules are followed.

1. Do not climb alone. Novices should climb with experienced climbers or join a club to learn and practice good technique.

2. Climb with proper equipment. Roped climbing at Devil's Lake requires a 120–150-foot climbing rope.

3. When top roping put in a minimum of three separate anchors. When climbing on ropes you have not set up, make sure the rope is correctly set up. Check anchors and slings frequently for dislodgment and wear.

4. Develop a "feel" for the friction on Devil's Lake quartzite. Remember that wet rocks, particularly when lichen-covered, are virtually frictionless.

5. Be aware that wasps may be encountered at any time except during the winter months.

6. Do not dislodge rocks. If rocks are accidentally dislodged and fall, warn those below by calling "rock." Try to discourage thoughtless persons from throwing rocks.

7. Learn to recognize poison ivy, because this plant grows in abundance near some trails and climbing areas.

# The East Bluff

The climbing areas at Devil's Lake State Park are divided by the lake into the East Bluff and the West Bluff. Both bluffs consist largely of typical alpine talus about 400 feet high, made of rocks ranging in size from small boulders to some as large as a room. Most climbing is done on the broken-up summit cliffs above the talus. In some areas rock outcroppings also appear on the lower slopes, for example, along the railroad tracks on the east shore.

The Devil's Lake quartzite has poor friction at best and hardly any when wet. This is especially true where the rocks are lichen-covered. On sunny days the warm rocks will be covered by swarming wasps. Their nests are usually found in cracks; climbers beware. Another inhabitant of smaller cracks are bats; they, and pigeons flushed out of larger cracks and chimneys, occasionally give the climber a scare. There is also an abundance of poison ivy in the park.

The East Bluff, by popular convention, is the entire bluff extending south along the east shore of the lake, turning east at Balanced Rock and extending 2.5 miles eastward to Highway 113.

Parking is available at the south shore picnic area and at the beginning of the CCC Trail .5 mile east. The park is very crowded during the summer months.

Three good trails reach up the talus to the top of the bluff: Balanced Rock Trail, Potholes Trail, and CCC Trail. No official trails reach the top of the bluff east of the CCC Trail. An unofficial trail begins near the Group Camp road east of the CCC parking area and ends at the Ice Age Trail. Farther east on the Sandstone Bluff there are climbers' trails. Of course, it is possible to reach any part of the bluff by going up boulderfields or the wooded slopes.

East Bluff, Sandstone Bluff. Photo: Sven Olof Swartling.

East Bluff, East of the Quarry Rocks. Photo: Sven Olof Swartling.

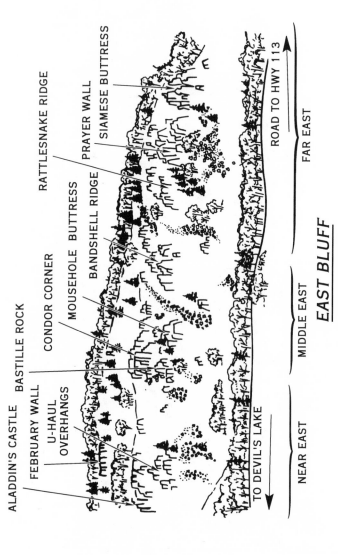

ALADDIN'S CASTLE   BASTILLE ROCK

FEBRUARY WALL   CONDOR CORNER   RATTLESNAKE RIDGE

U-HAUL   MOUSEHOLE BUTTRESS   PRAYER WALL
OVERHANGS   BANDSHELL RIDGE   SIAMESE BUTTRESS

**EAST BLUFF**

EAST OF THE QUARRY ROCKS, EAST SECTION

TO DEVIL'S LAKE

NEAR EAST   MIDDLE EAST   FAR EAST

ROAD TO HWY 113

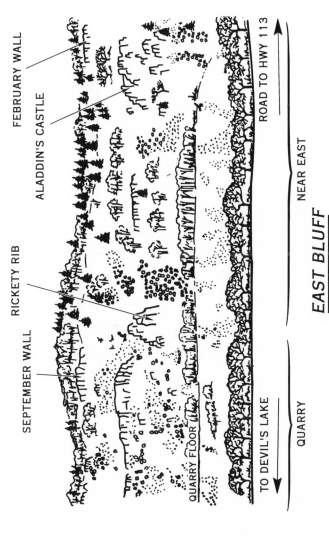

FEBRUARY WALL

ALADDIN'S CASTLE

RICKETY RIB

SEPTEMBER WALL

QUARRY FLOOR

TO DEVIL'S LAKE

QUARRY

NEAR EAST

ROAD TO HWY 113

## EAST BLUFF

EAST OF THE QUARRY ROCKS, WEST SECTION

45

East Bluff, West of the Quarry Rocks. Photo: Sven Olof Swartling.

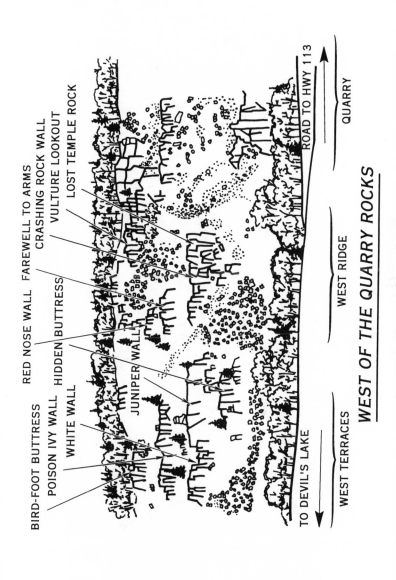

BIRD-FOOT BUTTRESS
RED NOSE WALL  FAREWELL TO ARMS
POISON IVY WALL  HIDDEN BUTTRESS  CRASHING ROCK WALL
WHITE WALL  VULTURE LOOKOUT
JUNIPER WALL  LOST TEMPLE ROCK

ROAD TO HWY 113

TO DEVIL'S LAKE

WEST TERRACES  WEST RIDGE  QUARRY

## WEST OF THE QUARRY ROCKS

East Bluff, East Rampart. Photo: Chuck Koch.

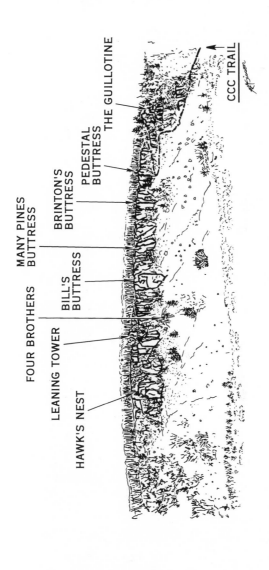

FOUR BROTHERS

LEANING TOWER

HAWK'S NEST

MANY PINES
BUTTRESS

BRINTON'S
BUTTRESS

BILL'S
BUTTRESS

PEDESTAL
BUTTRESS

THE GUILLOTINE

CCC TRAIL

## *EAST BLUFF*

EAST RAMPART

49

East Bluff, West End. Photo: Chuck Koch.

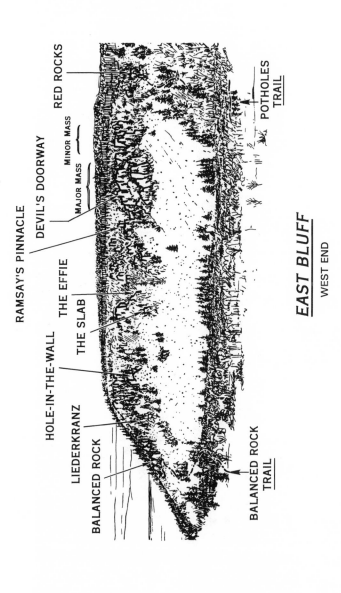

RAMSAY'S PINNACLE

DEVIL'S DOORWAY

RED ROCKS

MINOR MASS

MAJOR MASS

POTHOLES TRAIL

HOLE-IN-THE-WALL

THE EFFIE

THE SLAB

LIEDERKRANZ

BALANCED ROCK

BALANCED ROCK TRAIL

## EAST BLUFF

WEST END

East Bluff, Railroad Tracks. Photo: Sven Olof Swartling.

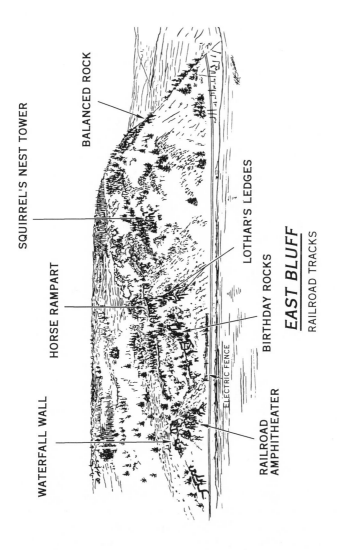

SQUIRREL'S NEST TOWER

BALANCED ROCK

HORSE RAMPART

WATERFALL WALL

LOTHAR'S LEDGES

BIRTHDAY ROCKS

ELECTRIC FENCE

RAILROAD AMPHITHEATER

*EAST BLUFF*

RAILROAD TRACKS

# Major Rock Groups of the East Bluff

Near the eastern end of the East Bluff, 2.5 miles east of Devil's Lake, is Sandstone Bluff, a summit band .4 mile long. Moving west, the next group of outcroppings is East of the Quarry Rocks, consisting of small outcroppings scattered across the upper half of the bluff. West of the quarry, is West of the Quarry Rocks, a group of relatively small outcroppings covering the entire height of the bluff.

NOTE: *The quarry itself is closed to public use.*

East of the upper portion of the CCC Trail, is a group of outcroppings called The Guillotine. West of The Guillotine is East Rampart, an almost continuous band of summit buttresses having the highest concentration of climbs. It is the most popular climbing area.

After a break in the summit band, the cliff resumes west of the Potholes Trail with the largest and most expansive cliff area, Doorway Rocks, which includes the spectacular Devil's Doorway. Continuing westward the outcroppings are discontinuous until Balanced Rock Wall, named after a large boulder perched near the edge. The bluff then turns abruptly north and follows the shore line.

Viewed from the west side of the lake, the northern leg of the East Bluff has a pronounced diagonal decline to the north. It is made up of several distinct bands. The lower, southern, rock bands are the major structures of climbing interest. They are (south to north) Lothar's Ledges, Horse Rampart, Birthday Rocks, Lumby Ridge, and Railroad Amphitheater. At the north end of the lake are a few small outcroppings: Monolith Blocks, Tomahawk Rocks, and Elephant Rocks.

In general, there is little difference between climbing on either the East Bluff or the West Bluff, with the exception of the Sandstone Bluff. The greater concentration of longer, difficult climbs and the well-developed trail system from the CCC Trail westward tend to draw more climbers. The scattering of the rock groups east of the CCC Trail and on the West Bluff, combined with the limited trail system, makes the climbing areas more difficult to locate and therefore less frequented. It should be recognized that, personal prejudice aside, climbing on either bluff can be equally challenging.

focus of the route is a large quartzite pebble on the face.

**4**   CHEZ'S CHIMNEY, 5.4. Obvious chimney.

The following three routes (5–7) have the same start.

**5**   TEAM ARTURO, 5.10b. Climb to the left side of the roof, move up and left, making use of the crescent-shaped crack, continue straight up to top, staying left of the pebbles.
*Variation,* ARTURO DIRECT, 5.10b. Climb crack 5 feet right of Chez's Chimney (route 4). Joins Team Arturo at upper crack.

**6**   ALLIGATOR WALL, 5.9. Climb to left side of roof, at roof level, step up and right over roof. Continue up and slightly left on the embedded quartzite pebbles.

**7**   DANCING MADLY BACKWARDS, 5.10b. Climb to left side of roof, traverse right to end of roof, step up and left over roof onto some pebbles. Continue up and slightly left to a difficult finish.
*Variation,* 5.11c. Start directly below right end of roof.

**8**   CURVING CRACK, 5.8. Crack curving slightly right, the hardest move is at the top.

**9**   DECEPTIVE, 5.10c/10d. Start a few feet right of Curving Crack (route 8) on small, sharp flakes. Climb up and slightly right to a rest spot, then straight up, finishing just right of the top of Curving Crack.

**10**   OUT THERE, 5.9. Start near dirty chimney, climb straight up to small overhang at 20 feet. Continue up and right past several flakes, finish at tree.

**11**   FREAKY FACE, 5.8–5.10d. A steep clean face with several variations in route and difficulty.

**12**   5.7. Climb crack in inside corner. When crack ends 10 feet below top, climb rounded corner to top.

**13**   SEPSEN WALL, 5.12a/12b. Climb through obvious notch in overhang, continue up and slightly left on wall above.

**14**   UBERSCHMITT, 5.12b. Start up Tarantula (route 15), pull up over right end of big overhang, continue on wall above.

**15**   TARANTULA, 5.10b. Start in inside corner, use under-

Curving Crack (diagram 1 E, route 8). Climber: David Harrison.
Photo: Sven Olof Swartling.

clings to exit left around roof and up to big overhang. Finger traverse right to join Gargantua (route 16).

**16** GARGANTUA, 5.10b. Climb crack in this nice-looking roof to an easier crack leading almost to the top, finish on short face.

*Variation,* 5.9. Avoids the roof. Start right of corner, same as Baker Street (route 17), traverse left above roof to Gargantua crack, continue up.

**17** BAKER STREET, 5.10d. Start right of corner, follow thin crack up and slightly left to face above with small, sharp holds. Don't get to close to Gargantua (route 16).

**18** PACIFIC OCEAN WALL, 5.11d. Ascend shallow scoop. A hard pull leads to more difficult climbing in the thin groove above.

**19** SEVEN SEAS, 5.11b. Climb right of Pacific Ocean Wall (route 18). A lunge to a jug hold on the corner is needed. Avoid the tree.

**20** AMERICAN BEAUTY CRACK, 5.8. Slightly overhanging, off-width crack.

**21** EVERLEIGH CLUB CRACK, 5.8. Finger-sized layback crack left of gully.

**22** 5.9. Start climbing in dihedral, exit left and finish on wall above.

**23** 5.7. Crack.

**24** 5.8. Crack.

**25** PTOOEY, 5.8. An interesting and awkward crack in the inside corner. It tends to spit the climber out rather quickly.

**26** THREE CHOICES, 5.8–5.10a. Start from top of boulder, climb 15 feet to diagonal ledge. Choose one of the finishes below.

5.10a. Follow ledge up and left to corner, then straight up to top.

5.9. Continue climbing straight up face.

5.8. Climb face, staying a few feet right.

**27** HALF CRACK, 5.7. Climb halfway up crack, continue over flakes straight to top.

*Variation,* 5.6. Follow crack to top.

**28** BASS TREE, 5.3. Wide crack.

**29** TEN-ISH SHOES, 5.10a. Climb corner right of Bass Tree (route 28).

**30**      EIGHT PLUS, 5.8. Climb over flaky central section of face to small overhang, pass overhang on the left.

**31**      BROKEN FOOT, 5.4. Wide diagonal crack.

**32**      DOWN UNDER, 5.9. Start climb 2 to 3 feet right of Broken Foot (route 31), climb straight up past a couple of small overhangs, using underclings.

**33**      SHIN BONE, 5.10b. You'll have bleeding shins if you slip. Climb as close to corner as possible.


## NEW SANDSTONE AREA (No Diagram)

APPROACH: From Old Sandstone Area parking area, continue east .4 mile to a small parking area on the north side of the road (approximately .25 mile west of Highway 113). Walk west 150 feet along the road to a faint trail leading up and west to the overhanging rock outcropping. The hanging dihedral at the left (west) end is named Donkey Dihedral. The climbs are described from west to east.

**1**      LASER BEAM, 5.11b. Climb thin right-curving groove in smooth wall, finish in jam crack.

**2**      DONKEY DIHEDRAL, 5.12b/12c. Located 31 feet right (east) of Laser Beam (route 1). Climb through first overhang on good holds, continue with crotch-splitting stems to reach easier climbing to top.

**3**      SHAKING HANDS WITH THE CHIMP, 5.13a. Located 30 feet right (east) of Donkey Dihedral (route 2). Climb up and left to arete, then up arete for 10 feet to where a long stretch across a blank slab leads to an overhanging groove. (Enjoy the swing if you come off.) Continue up groove to roof and finally up crack to top.

**4**      KINGSBURY NON-ALCOHOLIC ARETE, 5.12b. Climb arete left of Kingsbury Cruise (route 5).

**5**      KINGSBURY CRUISE, 5.11a. Climb overhanging crack to bulge (crux) and up to final roof. Finish directly over roof.

**6**      WET PAPER BAG, 5.10d. Located 8 feet right (east) of Kingsbury Cruise (route 5). Layback up to overhanging crack, exit right at the roof.

**7**  THIN TIPS, B1. Located 7 feet right (east) of Wet Paper Bag (route 6). Climb bulge.

There is a low level traverse starting left of Donkey Dihedral (route 2) and ending right of Thin Tips (route 7).

## East of the Quarry Rocks

Climbs in East of the Quarry Rocks are located east of the worked quarry area. *No climbs are in the worked quarry.* All of the quarried area, including the quarry floor, is closed to *all* public use.

East of the Quarry Rocks extends east 1,200 feet past the quarry. Rock outcroppings are found along most of this section of bluff. They fall into several bands, with one band considerably more prominent than the others. The main band is interrupted twice by open slopes about 100 feet wide, conveniently dividing the rocks into three major subsections: Far East, Middle East, and Near East. There is also a separate Summit Band.

APPROACH: Hiking in East of the Quarry Rocks is one of the more disagreeable activities at Devil's Lake, particularly in the summer. Therefore, climbing has generally been confined to the spring and fall seasons. The Far East and Middle East are generally reached by hiking up from the road. A few cars can be parked on the north side of the road, .9 mile east of the CCC parking area. The easternmost outcropping of Far East, the Siamese Buttress, comes into view as you go farther east along the road. The Near East is also reached by hiking up from the road. A couple of small parking areas are located .7 mile east of the CCC parking area, one on the north side and one on the south side of the road.

# Major Rock Groups of East of the Quarry Rocks

*Far East*

Siamese Buttress consists of two narrow buttresses separated by a steep couloir.

Prayer Wall is the most prominent rock outcropping in Far East. The southeast-facing vertical wall has several excellent climbs.

Rattlesnake Ridge. There are short climbs on the east flank of the ridge, the side with the greatest relief.

Bandshell Ridge. The area is named for the semicircular rock outcropping below the major outcropping. Unfortunately, it is composed of close-layered, highly fractured rock, and therefore not climbed. The climbing is concentrated on a pair of buttresses 35 feet high, with a chimney complex tucked between them. This complex, The Gullet, is the distinctive feature of the area.

*Middle East*

Mousehole Buttress is part of the lower level of the Middle East. The buttress has a few 60-foot, easy routes interrupted by a large bench.

Condor Corner is located on the upper level of Middle East, three-quarters of the way up the bluff. The oversized corner of this 40-foot wall is its most striking feature.

Bastille Rock is located almost directly below Condor Corner and is not a particularly eye-appealing outcropping. The central (highest) part has a few 35-foot climbs.

*Near East*

Aladdin's Castle is the upper western outcropping of Near East. It can be seen when one is level with the eastern end of the quarry floor. A 40-foot inside corner is its prominent feature.

U-Haul Overhangs is the lower and easternmost outcropping of Near East. The climbs are on two small formations, 80 feet apart at roughly the same level. The western formation is 30 feet high and slightly overhung. It has two distinctive cracks 3 feet apart, with a large boulder under the right crack.

Rickety Rib is an impressive 40-foot buttress well hidden in the trees near the eastern edge of the quarry. This small area is difficult to reach, since the quarry floor has been closed to public use. There is no climbing description for this area.

## Far East

The easiest way to locate climbing areas in the Far East and Middle East is to hike to Siamese Buttress and then traverse west from buttress to buttress. Refer to the elevation drawing of East of the Quarry Rocks, East Section, for the relative location of the buttresses.

### SIAMESE BUTTRESS (Diagram 2 E)

ACCESS: From a small parking area on the north side of the road, .9 mile east of the CCC parking area, ascend the bluff to reach the base of the buttress.

I  EAST SIAM, 5.4. Start from ledge, climb overhang, finish on face above.

2  HALFWAY, 5.5. Climb sub-buttress part way up gully on west side of East Siam (route 1).

3  WEST SIAM, 5.6. Start at southeast corner of buttress, right and below the platform. Climb groove to shattered rib, then to overhang, which is passed on the left.

4  SVEN GOLLY, 5.9. Start on southeast platform 15 feet

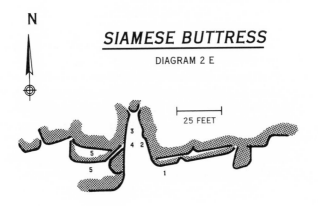

N

*SIAMESE BUTTRESS*

DIAGRAM 2 E

25 FEET

above base of buttress. Climb east side of prominent southeast corner, staying left of groove.

**5**    THREE STEP, 5.8. Climb center of face with two wide ledges.


## BAD NEWS GULLY (No Diagram)

Bad News Gully is located 75 feet west of Siamese Buttress and forms its western boundary. The name reflects its character—narrow, steep, and dirty. There are a couple of climbs halfway up the gully, on the west side. West of the gully there is a rather complex section of short slabs and walls.


## PRAYER WALL (Diagram 3 E)

ACCESS: From Siamese Buttress, traverse 225 feet west, past Bad News Gully, and ascend 100 feet to base of Prayer Wall.

**1**    THE ROOK, 5.8. Climb narrow face left of jam crack, This Is a Six? (route 2). There are some long reaches on small sharp holds. Easier than it looks.

**2**    THIS IS A SIX?, 5.6. Jam crack that is harder than it looks.

**3**    SICKLE, 5.10d/11a. Start climb behind large oak tree. Climb face and shallow crack to left end of curved slot. From slot, follow crack to top.

**4**    BISHOP, 5.7. Climb follows the long, left-slanting crack. An attractive route with continuous 5.7 climbing.
*Variation,* 5.11b. Start farther left, climb face and join crack at 20 feet.

**5**    PRAYER WHEEL, 5.11b/11c. Start just left of inside corner and climb straight up to triangular pocket at 15 feet; continue on wall above to top of summit block. Avoid using the right edge holds halfway up.

**6**    THE PAWN, 5.4. Climb inside corner and slab. At 20 feet switch to crack on left wall, finish right of summit block.

# PRAYER WALL

DIAGRAM 3 E

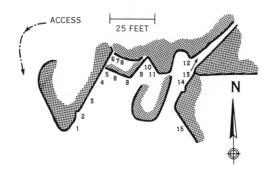

**7** 5.6. Climb overhang on upper wall just right of grungy-looking chimney.

**8** BUDDHA, 5.8. Climb crack in middle of bulge or climb right corner to middle ledge with one large block; continue on center of wall above.

**9** MAGELLANIC CLOUD, 5.11d. Climb lower face 6 feet left of Close Call (route 10). Thin cracks lead to better holds. Joins Buddha (route 8) at ledge.

**10** CLOSE CALL, 5.6. A well-defined inside corner.

**11** PRAYER FLAG, 5.7. Crack in southwest face, right of inside corner. Joins Close Call (route 10) halfway up.

**12** NO VACANCY, 5.8. Start climb 25 feet above base platform. Climb crack past overhang, finish in groove above right side of overhang.

**13** VACANT, 5.10a. Start climb 25 feet above base platform. Climb center and upper right side of narrow face. Avoid using right corner near top.
*Variation*, 5.11b. Same start; then climb left side of upper face.

**14** 5.9. Start from block in gully, climb 20-foot face left of broken chimney.

**15** 5.4. A 30-foot face route ending halfway up buttress.

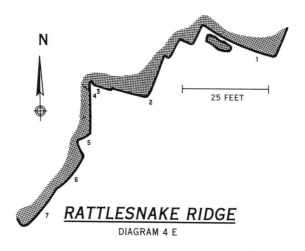

## RATTLESNAKE RIDGE (Diagram 4 E)

ACCESS: From the lowest eastern point of Prayer Wall traverse 100 feet west to Rattlesnake Ridge.

1   THE RATTLE, 5.5. Climb face, pass 3-foot square flake 10 feet above the ground on the right.
    *Variation,* 5.8. Climb over flake, or stay left. Caution, the flake is loose!
2   RIGHT NOSE, 5.5. Climb, staying close to corner.
3   LEFT NOSE, 5.6. Climb just left of corner.
4   TIMBER SNAKE, 5.9. Thin joint on lower wall left of V-chimney.
5   SNAKE SKIN, 5.6. Start from niche, climb crack that slants slightly right.
6   5.8. Start in center of wall, climb up and right to crack, then back left to top.
7   5.6. Climb crack in left part of wall.

## BANDSHELL RIDGE (Diagram 5 E)

ACCESS: The easiest way to reach Bandshell Ridge is by traversing diagonally 175 feet up and west, from the lowest blocks of Rattlesnake Ridge.

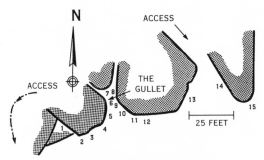

## BANDSHELL RIDGE

DIAGRAM 5 E

**I**  5.9. Start from ledge, climb left side of wall.

**2**  LARGO, 5.8. South corner of west buttress. A long reach is helpful.

**3**  ENCORE, 5.8. Climb southeast face and crack straight up to top of buttress. Another long reach route.

**4**  FINE TUNING, 5.8. Climb 15 feet to a 6-foot right-slanting crack. Use bucket hold in crack for one move, then climb straight up to top.
*Variation,* 5.7. At 15 feet, follow right-slanting crack.

**5**  MINUET, 5.4. Climb blocky crack and wall.

**6**  THE GULLET, 5.5. Climb the 5-foot-wide gap by stemming. Some people prefer to face in, others prefer to face out.

**7**  TUBA, 5.11b. Overhang inside gullet.

**8**  5.6. East wall of gullet.

**9**  ARM OVERTURE, 5.6. Jam crack 8 feet right of The Gullet (route 6).

**10**  5.6. Climb crack 5 feet right of Arm Overture (route 9).

**II**  5.5. Climb into small niche, continue on southwest corner of buttress.

**12**  FIRST MOVEMENT, 5.6. Start near small hickory tree and climb straight up to top.

**13**  TORN JOINT, 5.10d/11a. Climb center of face, aiming for vertical crack near top.
*Variation,* 5.9+. Same start, but traverse right and move up, using a couple of holds near right corner. Then traverse left to center of face, finish in vertical crack near top.

**14**   5.5. Climb broken southwest face and crack.

**15**   5.4. South corner of buttress.

## Middle East

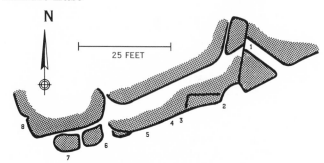

*MOUSEHOLE BUTTRESS*

DIAGRAM 6 E

## MOUSEHOLE BUTTRESS (Diagram 6 E)

ACCESS: From Bandshell Ridge, traverse west 100 feet across a small boulderfield to the buttress.

**1**   MOUSEHOLE, 5.5. Start in short chimney and climb crack leading out of chimney.

**2**   JERRY, 5.7. Climb corner to bench, continue in wide crack, finish on upper corner.

**3**   TOM, 5.7. Thin crack 4 feet right of Mouse Crack (route 4).

**4**   MOUSE CRACK, 5.7. Climb crack in lower wall to juniper tree on bench. On upper wall start at flake, then climb right or left past overhang.

**5**   TRAP, 5.11a. Face 4 feet left of Mouse Crack (route 4).

**6**   EAST PILLAR, 5.5. Climb east corner, finish on slab above.

**7**   WEST PILLAR, 5.6. Climb face of pillar, finish on slab above.

**8**   5.5. Crack 12 feet left of West Pillar (route 7). Climb crack or just right of crack.

Shooting Star (diagram 7 E, route 4). Climber: Alex Andrews. Photo: Sven Olof Swartling.

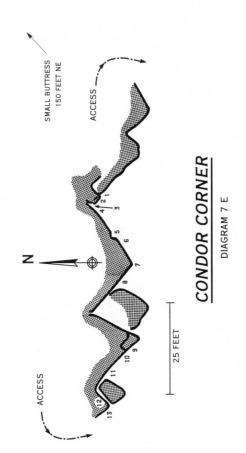

SMALL BUTTRESS
150 FEET NE

ACCESS

ACCESS

N

25 FEET

## *CONDOR CORNER*

DIAGRAM 7 E

## CONDOR CORNER (Diagram 7 E)

ACCESS: From the top of Mousehole Buttress, traverse 125 feet diagonally up and west to the base of Condor Corner. This area can also be reached from the Ice Age Trail along the top of the bluff. 150 feet east of February Wall descend a faint ridge to the top of Condor Corner. (Good Luck!)

**1**    5.4. Climb lower wall into a subsidiary inside corner. Several easy climbs are possible further right.

**2**    SALT PETER, 5.8. Climb hanging pillar and crack 2 to 4 feet right of Condor Corner (route 3).

**3**    CONDOR CORNER, 5.5. An impressive inside corner/ chimney.

**4**    SHOOTING STAR, 5.11d. Climb crack system in center of face. Near top, use bucket hold below left crack to move up and right. Climb overhanging crack and face above without using the right corner. This route ends at the high point of the buttress.
*Variation*, 5.11a. From bucket hold, climb left crack.

**5**    THE JOKER, 5.6. Climb past the block-filled niche to platform, finish on upper right corner.

**6**    PETE'S NEMESIS, 5.9. Climb thin crack 3 feet left of The Joker (route 5); avoid using holds near The Joker.

**7**    COSMIC, 5.10d. Climb corner. Getting off the ground is the crux.

**8**    GOT YOU, 5.8. Short jam or layback crack. A harder variation uses only the crack for holds.

**9**    5.5. Climb crack and upper corner.

**10**   5.8. Crack just left of route 9.

**11**   5.7. Climb crack to top.

**12**   5.7. Face. Avoid using tower behind, and your behind.

**13**   5.8. Face just left of corner behind a small pine tree.

## SMALL BUTTRESS 150 FEET NORTHEAST OF CONDOR CORNER (No Diagram)

**14**   5.5. Crack in south-southwest face.

**15**   5.6. South corner. Climb through open book halfway up.

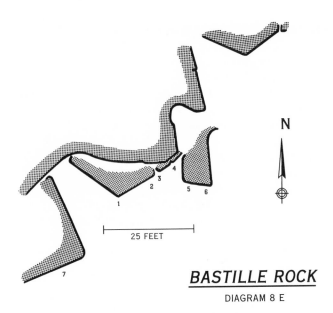

## BASTILLE ROCK

DIAGRAM 8 E

## BASTILLE ROCK (Diagram 8 E)

ACCESS: From the base of Mousehole Buttress, traverse west 100 feet. From Condor Corner, descend 100 feet.

1    LOUIS V, 5.5. Corner.
2    LOUIS VI, 5.6. Face and crack.
3    FENESTRATION, 5.6. Start in short chimney, climb to substantial ledge about midlevel; climb upper wall into a small, deep V-notch near top.
4    GINNY CREEPER, 5.6. Start 5 feet east of Fenestration (route 3). Climb lower crack into inside corner, right to corner ledge, then up just right of overhang. The pioneers of this route had to force their way through a drapery of Virginia creeper.
      *Variation*, 5.8. Climb overhang directly.
5    WARDEN I, 5.8. Slightly overhanging corner.
6    WARDEN II, 5.10a. Short overhang problem.
7    DEALER'S CHOICE, 5.2–5.4. Low wall just west of Louis V (route 1).

## Near East

In the Near East there are several smaller outcroppings on various levels, but moving around the area is a general nuisance. From the parking areas .7 mile east of the CCC parking area, follow the road east 400 feet. Ascend the bluff following the east edge of the scree slope formed by the quarry operation. When you are level with the quarry floor, you can see two outcroppings halfway up the bluff. Aladdin's Castle is the western outcropping. The outcropping east of it has a few 20-foot climbs. Farther west there are a few low rock outcroppings, but no worthwhile climbs.

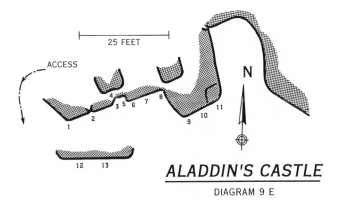

## *ALADDIN'S CASTLE*

DIAGRAM 9 E

## ALADDIN'S CASTLE (Diagram 9 E)

ACCESS: *From below*—From the eastern end of the quarry floor, walk straight up the bluff 350 feet. (*Avoid the quarry floor, which is closed to public use.*) *From above*—From the base of February Wall, descend straight down to Aladdin's Castle.

**1**    SECOND WISH, 5.7. Corner with small overhang at 12 feet.

**2**    FLYING CARPET, 5.7. Crack with two small V-niches. Careful, you may go for a ride.

**3**    5.4. Start in V-chimney, continue in inside corner to large platform.

**4**    SZHAZAM, 5.8. From platform, climb short tricky face, without use of the left corner, to top of the lower (western) high point.

**5**    THE LAMP, 5.5. A longer chimney/crack route. Start near route 3, climb up and right, finish to the right of lower high point.

**6**    5.7. Start climb in cracks on lower face, continue on rib to small pine tree.

**7**    FIRST MAKE A WISH, 5.8. A quarter-inch crack that can be identified by a pinch hold 10 feet up. Don't take this line lightly; the difficulty is not apparent at first glance.

**8**    THREE WISHES, 5.6. Start in inside corner below the higher (eastern) high point; about 20 feet up there are three ways to continue:

(1) 5.6. Chimney left of the eastern high point.

(2) 5.10c. Rounded corner.

(3) 5.5. Steep ramp leading up and right.

**9**    GENIE, 5.10a. A rounded corner leading to a ledge below the eastern high point.

**10**    FIRST WISH, 5.10b. Climb face right of Genie (route 9); avoid using the right corner.

*Variation*, 5.10d. Climb face without using the two large holds near the corner.

**11**    5.6. Start climb in short crack, continue on corner above.

**12–13**    THIRD WISH, 5.6–5.7. Two short crack routes on lower wall.

The rock outcroppings east of Aladdin's Castle have a few short climbs.

## U-HAUL OVERHANGS (Diagram 10 E)

ACCESS: From the eastern end of the quarry floor, traverse diagonally up (northeast) 200 feet to reach base of outcropping. (*The quarry floor is closed to public use.*)

**1**    FREE MILEAGE, 5.7. Start at lowest point of south wall between the boulder and corner; at 15 feet, continue on east wall.

**2**    BUDGET, 5.6. Crack with good jam holds. Easy in spite

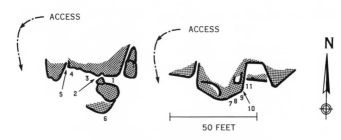

## U-HAUL OVERHANGS

DIAGRAM 10 E

of being overhung. More challenging if you avoid using the boulder.

**3** HURTS, 5.8. Continuously overhanging crack with good holds most of the way.

*Variation,* 5.10a. Climb left of Hurts without using the crack.

**4** AVIS, 5.8. Climb wall just right of corner to ledge 20 feet up, continue to top on corner or move right on ledge to crack.

**5** RENT-A-WRECK, 5.5. Chimney at west end of wall.

**6** 5.7. Short climb on lower east wall.

**7** 5.6. Climb center crack and inside corner on left side of pillar.

**8** NOSE, NOSE, ANYTHING GOES, 5.8. Climb face straight up below hanging corner, continue on corner to top.

**9** WE TRY HARDER, 5.8. Start on east corner, at 10 feet step left onto lip of overhang, finish on face above.

**10** . . . AND HARDER, 5.10c. Same start as We Try Harder (route 9); at 10 feet step right. Finish on corner and crack right of corner.

**11** BANANA PEEL, 5.10a. Climb up and right on sloping ramp to upper overhang. Pass overhang on left, then follow corner to top.

# Summit Band

The Summit Band consists of two low walls located near the top of the bluff, September Wall and February Wall. September Wall, well above the eastern edge of the quarry, can be seen from below, though practically hidden by trees.

APPROACH: *Western Cwm boulderfield from the Group Camp area*—Ascend the wooded bluff along a trail which starts directly across the road from the Group Camp road 500 feet east of the CCC parking area. When the trail fades, continue north through the woods 200 feet to the Ice Age Trail near an obvious low point in the Ice Age Trail. Walk 1,200 feet east along the trail to a clearing at the top of the bluff; the Western Cwm boulderfield is located below this clearing. *Western Cwm boulderfield from the CCC Trail*—Take the CCC Trail to the top of the bluff. Above D'Arcy's Wall walk north through the woods 250 feet to the East Bluff Woods Trail. Follow the trail east 350 feet to where it joins the Ice Age Trail. Continue east 2,000 feet to the Western Cwm boulderfield.

## SEPTEMBER WALL (Diagram II E)

ACCESS: September Wall is located 1,000 feet east of the Western Cwm boulderfield. Just before a short, left-turning, uphill section, leave the trail and follow a faint trail 150 feet south.

I    HICKORY LEFT, 5.10a. Climb thin crack.
2    HICKORY RIGHT, 5.9. Start in shallow inside corner, finish slightly left of nose.
3    5.8. Face 4–5 feet right of Hickory Right (route 2). Balance up on small ramp a few feet above the ground. Continue up and slightly right to top.
4    EQUINOX, 5.5. Climb right-slanting crack.
     *Variation*, 5.8. Climb just right of crack; avoid holds in or on the edge of the crack.
5    LABOR DAY, 5.7. Climb face to crack starting 8 feet up. Follow crack to top.
     *Variation*, 5.8. Start 5 feet farther left.
6    IN STEP, 5.8. Start under overhang. Climb, passing overhang on right or left, continue just right of corner to top.

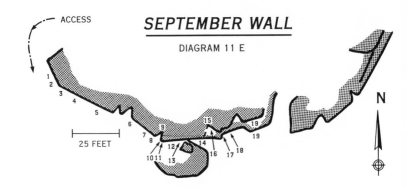

## SEPTEMBER WALL

### DIAGRAM 11 E

**7** FALL IS NEAR, 5.7. Interesting crack.

**8** PHIL'S NOSE, 5.10a. Climb corner to top.

**9** 5.4. Deep inside corner.

**10** LADY AND THE TRAMP, 5.11b. Start on narrow face left of End of September (route 11), at 10 feet move left around corner to overhanging crack.

**11** END OF SEPTEMBER, 5.9. Corner. Requires a long reach.

**12** 5.10d. Face between End of September (route 11) and The Fang (route 13). Start at center of face, climb up and slightly left, ending at the top of End of September.

**13** THE FANG, 5.9. Left-curving jam crack.

**14** 5.7. Climb to top of hanging inside corner, continue in diagonal crack.

**15** 5.5. Inside corner.

**16** QUEEN OF HEARTS, 5.10b. A very nice face route on thin holds.

**17** THE CHOPPER, 5.8. Climb inside corner to platform below overhang, follow crack up and slightly left to top.
*Variation,* 5.7. Move right at overhang and climb over wobbly block.

**18** SON OF CHOPPER, 5.10d. Start on first ledge 12 feet up, climb face and corner to wobbly block. This route is 4 to 6 feet right of The Chopper (route 17).

**19** BEHIND THE PINE, 5.7. Climb crack in lower flaky face to ledge. Move left on ledge and step up on small foothold behind pine tree to instant exposure, continue straight up on face.

## FEBRUARY WALL (Diagram 12 E)

ACCESS: February Wall is 800 feet east of the September Wall turnoff. Turn south just before a short, left-turning, uphill section and walk 50 feet to the outcropping.

1   FEBRUARY 29, 5.9. Start in shallow inside corner, climb close to corner, finish just left of top overhang.

2   FEBRUARY 28, 5.10b. A straighter line. Climb middle of face and finish in notch of overhang.

3   DOUBLE FIN, 5.8. Start climb in thin crack just left of Flying Fish (route 4), follow zigzag cracks to top.

4   FLYING FISH, 5.8. A wide crack system whose offset cracks are harder than they look.

5   FISH FACE, 5.8. Face 4 feet right of Flying Fish (route 4). Climb face straight to top.

6   STRIDE RIGHT, 5.9. Nice face route. Same start as Fish Face (route 5). Climb up and slightly right to small overhang, then to top.

7   LEAP YEAR, 5.7. Start just left of corner and climb straight to top, passing overhang on left.
*Variation 1*, 5.7. Same start; at 10 feet step right onto lip of overhang, follow corner to top.
*Variation 2*, 5.8. Climb overhanging corner directly.

8   5.5. Crack.

9   5.5. Crack system and shallow inside corner.

10   TURNCOAT, 5.10a. Corner.

11   5.7. Start 3 feet right of corner, finish on ledge.

12   5.5. Face.

13   5.4. Chimney.

14   MINOR TECHNICALITY, B1. Climb face just left of Bread and Jam (route 15) on very thin holds, finish in crack.

15   BREAD AND JAM, 5.7. Climb diagonal crack without using right corner.

16   5.4. Corner.

17   5.4. Crack, joins corner at top.

18–20   5.4. Three easy cracks.

21   5.5. Face route.

22   5.6. Corner.

23   5.4. Crack.

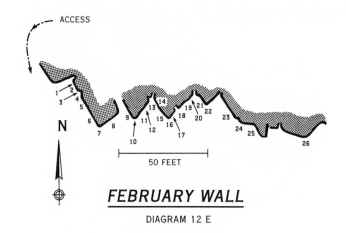

**FEBRUARY WALL**

DIAGRAM 12 E

**24**  5.6. Start on corner 4 feet right of crack, finish in groove.
**25**  PHOOEY, 5.8. Inside corner with overhanging crack at top.
**26**  5.4. Corner.

## West of the Quarry Rocks

INTRODUCTION

The rock outcroppings west of the quarry, West Ridge, Vulture Lookout, and West Terraces, are separated by three large boulderfields.

Two boulderfields start at road level and are connected at the very bottom of the bluff in a line of trees. The eastern boulderfield reaches up between West Ridge and West Terraces and provides relatively easy access to the top of the bluff. The western boulderfield reaches up west of West Terraces.

The third boulderfield, the Western Cwm, is located on the upper third of the bluff, above and west of the worked quarry. It separates the upper part of West Ridge (Red Nose Wall) from Vulture Lookout.

The rock outcropping above the western part of the quarry that is visible from the road offers no climbing. A small outcropping on the upper part of the bluff, between West Ridge and West Terraces, has a couple of climbs.

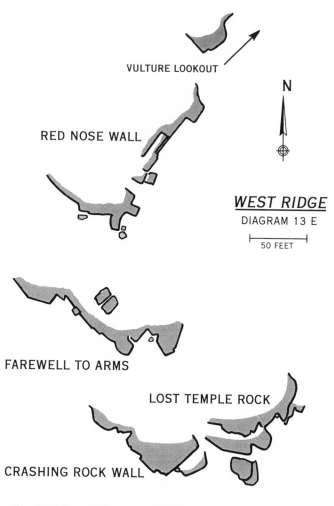

VULTURE LOOKOUT

RED NOSE WALL

N

**_WEST RIDGE_**
DIAGRAM 13 E

├──────┤
50 FEET

FAREWELL TO ARMS

LOST TEMPLE ROCK

CRASHING ROCK WALL

## West Ridge (Diagram 13 E)

APPROACH: From the CCC parking area, walk east on the paved road 1,000 feet almost to the bridge that crosses an old quarry road. After the bridge the road begins descending the moraine slope. Turn left, and walk northeast through the woods to a boulderfield, then up along the eastern edge of the boulderfield. A low rock outcropping can be seen above (unnamed). Crashing Rock Wall is located above this low rock outcropping, behind some trees. The upper part of West Ridge (Red Nose

Wall) is located along the western edge of the Western Cwm boulderfield and can be reached from the Ice Age Trail above. See Summit Band for this approach.

## CRASHING ROCK WALL (Diagram 14 E)

ACCESS: See Diagram 13 E, West Ridge.

1   THE EASEL, 5.9. Face route.
2   5.4. Crack system passing small pine in center of wall.
3   5.4. Crack system with birch bushes.
4   THE BLACKBOARD, 5.10b. Smooth face below high point of buttress.
5   5.3. Climb just west of corner. A longer route than most climbs in the area. Some loose rock high up.
6   5.5. Crack system.
7   5.5. Crack system.
8   5.8. Climb face and continue up overhang.
9   5.7. Corner.
10  5.7. Crack. Climb up and right to groove.

## LOST TEMPLE ROCK (Diagram 14 E)

ACCESS: See Diagram 13 E, West Ridge.

11  FURIOUS FUNNEL, 5.8. Climb lower wall to ledge at 15 feet, continue up from left end of ledge into the Furious Funnel right of block (a short chimney formed by a projecting block). Continue climbing just left of, and as close as possible to, the corner.
12  5.7. Start in short crack near center of amphitheater and climb to the same ledge as Furious Funnel (route 11), continue up steep gully with loose rock to top.
13  NEMESIS, 5.8. Start on left side of corner pedestal, continue straight up steep face, finish on ledge right and above pointed overhang.
14  LOST TEMPLE CORNER, 5.6. Start climb on right side of pedestal, continue in prominent inside corner. From the obvious resting ledge, follow crack to top.

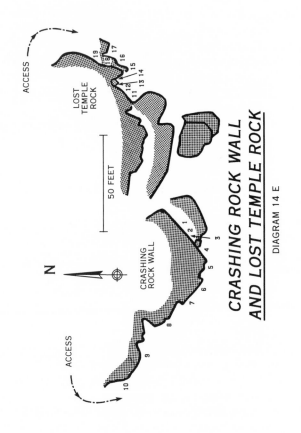

**N**

50 FEET

ACCESS

ACCESS

CRASHING ROCK WALL

LOST TEMPLE ROCK

*CRASHING ROCK WALL*
*AND LOST TEMPLE ROCK*

DIAGRAM 14 E

**15** FAITH, HOPE, AND TENSION, 5.8. Southeast corner. Start a few feet right of corner, traverse left to corner as soon as possible, follow corner to top.

*Variation,* 5.10c. Start from left of corner with a jump move.

**16** THE DOOM, 5.10b. Start up slight groove, climb over right end of overhang to ledge.

*Variation,* FATE, 5.11a/11b. Climb groove, passing lower overhang on left.

**17** 5.5. Climb short inside corner with deep crack to ledge.

**18** 5.6. Start from ledge, climb crack left of offset in wall.

**19** 5.6. Start from ledge, climb crack right of offset in wall.

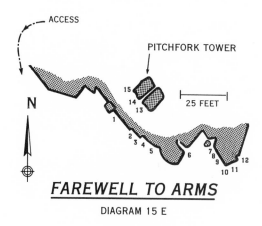

**FAREWELL TO ARMS**

DIAGRAM 15 E

## FAREWELL TO ARMS (Diagram 15 E)

ACCESS: See Diagram 13 E, West Ridge.

**1** ANNE'S 8, 5.6. Crack leading toward large pine tree at top.

**2** FAREWELL TO ARMS, 5.8. Start climb in inside lay-back corner, continue in crack above overhang.

**3** SKIN GRAFT, 5.11b. Thin crack. Climb crack just left of corner.

**4** COUNT YOUR FINGERS, 5.8. Inside corner crack with very sharp edge.

**5**   5.7. Start 5 feet right of Count Your Fingers (route 4). Finish in crack above.

**6**   5.4. Corner and overhang.

**7**   5.5. Climb chimney, passing top block on right.

**8**   NO ONE BUT ME, 5.11c. Tight crack 3 feet left of route 9.

**9**   5.7. Jam crack.

**10**  KEYSTONE, 5.10b. Corner.

**11**  THIS IS HARD!, 5.11b. Climb crack in center of face.

**12**  5.5. Climb chimney and crack.
        *Variation*, 5.7. Climb right rounded corner of chimney/crack.

## PITCHFORK TOWER (Diagram 15 E)

**13**  5.4. Chimney.

**14**  5.6. Same start as route 13. At 8 feet step out of chimney and climb left corner and face to top.

**15**  PITCHFORK, 5.10d. Climb overhanging southwest corner.

## RED NOSE WALL (Diagram 16 E)

ACCESS: See Diagram 13 E, West Ridge.

**1**   DIRTY JIM'S CRACK, 5.7. Inside corner. Awkward.

**2**   WHITE WASP, 5.11a. Start under overhang below corner. Climb overhang, continue in inside corner just right of corner.

**3**   THE REVOLT OF THE NERDS, 5.6. Start in inside corner, continue in crack above.

**4**   ELIMINATION, 5.6. Climb crack.

**5**   5.10a. Face between Elimination (route 4) and A Girl Named Sue (route 6).

**6**   A GIRL NAMED SUE, 5.8. Climb face and shallow crack 8 feet left of inside corner. Avoid using cracks on either side.

**7**   JUDGMENT DAY, 5.11c. Climb face by a series of laybacks and long reaches.

# RED NOSE WALL

DIAGRAM 16 E

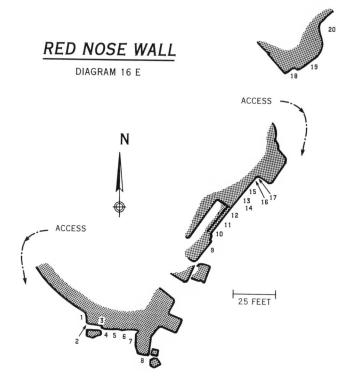

N

ACCESS

ACCESS

25 FEET

**8** 5.7. Start with layback, pass overhang on right or climb face below upper corner. Finish on southeast corner.

**9** VOYAGER, 5.11a. Climb upper wall left of Cutting Edge (route 10). Start with a layback, continue on upper, overhanging wall.

**10** CUTTING EDGE, 5.8. Climb the easy lower part of wall to overhanging diagonal crack 15 feet below top. Follow crack to top.

**11** SOLSTICE, 5.11c. Start on ledge and climb narrow face left of Bloodshed (route 12). Do not use Bloodshed crack.

**12** BLOODSHED, 5.7. Climb to ledge, then to inside corner. Pass both lower and upper overhangs on the left.

**13** WOUNDED KNEE, 5.10c. Climb to ledge. Continue up past a couple of small overhangs until upper corner is reached. Finish on right side of upper corner.

**14** LAUGHING SIOUX, 5.8. Same start as Wounded Knee

(route 13). Climb up and right onto small platform at 20 feet, finish in hanging inside corner.

**15** OCTOBER COUNTRY, 5.9+. Climb crack and a couple of downsloping projections. Very awkward.

**16** LOOK MA, NO HANDS, 5.10b. Overhanging wall and groove between October Country (route 15) and Breaking Away (route 17).

**17** BREAKING AWAY, 5.8. Climb inside corner. Watch for loose rocks.

**18** 5.5. Inside corner.

**19** 5.8. Climb crack system leading slightly left.

**20** NO PROBLEM, 5.10d. Climb flaring crack. Appears a lot easier than it is.

A number of short climbs and boulder problems can be found on the low walls above Red Nose Wall. The walls form a cirque above the Western Cwm boulderfield, almost connecting with Vulture Lookout to the east.


## VULTURE LOOKOUT (Diagram 17 E)

Well hidden by trees, Vulture Lookout is located 200 feet south of the Ice Age Trail, at the northeastern corner of the Western Cwm boulderfield. It is reached most easily from the Ice Age Trail.

APPROACH: *Western Cwm boulderfield from the Group Camp area*   Ascend the wooded bluff along a trail which starts directly across the road from the Group Camp road, 500 feet east of the CCC parking area. When the trail fades, continue north through the woods 200 feet to the Ice Age Trail near an obvious low point in the Ice Age Trail. Walk 1,200 feet east along the trail to a clearing at the top of the bluff; the Western Cwm boulderfield is located below this clearing. *Western Cwm boulderfield from the CCC Trail*   Take the CCC Trail to the top of the bluff. Above D'Arcy's Wall walk north through the woods 250 feet to the East Bluff Woods Trail. Follow the trail east 350 feet to where it joins the Ice Age Trail. Continue east 2,000 feet to the Western Cwm boulderfield.

# VULTURE LOOKOUT

DIAGRAM 17 E

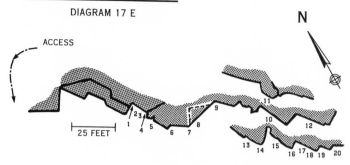

**1** MISSING PIECE, 5.7. Climb slightly overhanging inside corner to big platform, continue in crack to top.

**2** DURACELL, 5.10c. Start up vertical face, at 8 feet move left to crack.

**3** MAGIC MUSHROOM, 5.12b/12c. Climb vertical face straight to top. Beware of the tree when you fall.

**4** 5.7. Crack system slightly overhung at the start. Follow cracks straight to top.

**5** 5.6. Crack. This climb joins route 4 at 20 feet.

**6** DOUBLE JEOPARDY CRACKS, 5.9. Start in small inside corner, climb to ledge 12 feet up and rest, continue in left or right crack.

**7** THE ENERGIZER, 5.9. Start just right of corner. Climb up and left around corner to small overhang, move slightly left and follow crack (crux) to top.
*Variation*, 5.11a. Climb lower face just left of corner.

**8** THE V, 5.10d. Climb to alcove, then up and out of the V.

**9** 5.8. Crack to right of overhang.

**10** 5.7. Crack in center of wall.

**11** Two climbs on small tower with overhang.
5.8. Left corner.
5.10a. Thin cracks 6 feet right of corner.

**12** 5.8. Crack with small chockstone.

**13** HARDER BY THE CLIMBER, 5.6. Inside corner that has gotten harder after each climber.

**14** SPLIT CORNER, 5.7. Corner with crack.

**15** HIGH STEP, 5.11a. Short face and crack climb.

16   5.6. Inside corner.
17   TUBS, 5.9. Crack.
18   MOSS MUFFIN, 5.10b. Face and crack 3 feet right of
     Tubs (route 17).
19   5.6. Inside corner.
20   5.6. Inside corner.

← WEST POST 300 FEET

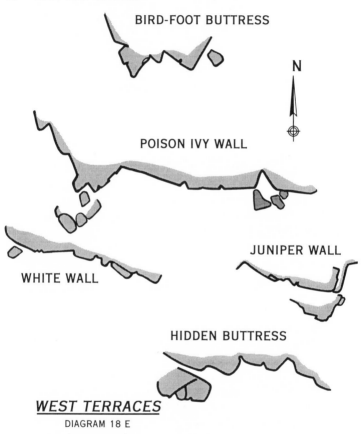

BIRD-FOOT BUTTRESS

N

POISON IVY WALL

JUNIPER WALL

WHITE WALL

HIDDEN BUTTRESS

**WEST TERRACES**
DIAGRAM 18 E

├─────────┤
   50 FEET

# West Terraces (Diagram 18 E)

APPROACH: From the CCC parking area, walk east on the paved road 1,000 feet to just before a bridge where the road crosses over an old quarry road and begins descending the moraine slope. Turn left and walk north through the trees to the base of a boulderfield which splits low down. The first terrace, Hidden Buttress, is just above the east margin of the western boulderfield behind a few trees.

## HIDDEN BUTTRESS (Diagram 19 E)

ACCESS: See Diagram 18 E, West Terraces.

1   5.7. Climb center of face.

2   CHARLIE BROWN, 5.6. Climb just right of southeast corner of buttress.

3   PEANUTS, 5.10a. Climb crack left of southeast corner of buttress.
    *Variation,* 5.8. At 10 feet, traverse left a few feet to another crack leading to a large ledge, continue near corner to top.

4   LINUS, 5.11b. Thin crack in center of face.

5   THE FERN, 5.10b. Climb lower face, 4 feet right of Nowhere Man (route 6), continue in crack above.

6   NOWHERE MAN, 5.11c/11d. Climb shallow groove/crack which ends 8 feet below top, continue straight up on face above.
    *Variation,* 5.8. Where groove/crack ends, traverse right 5 feet and follow crack to top.

7   PINE SAP, 5.9. A sticky corner.

8   5.8. Climb straight up near corner.

9   5.9. Face; avoid using corner.

10  5.5. Broken face.

11  5.10a. Climb overhang direct.

12  5.6. Climb to ledge under large ceiling, move right and up over overhang.

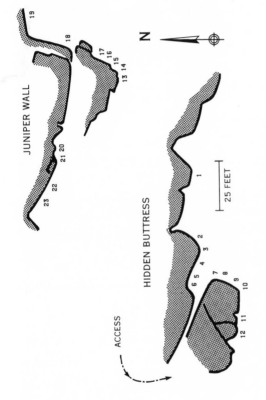

*HIDDEN BUTTRESS
AND JUNIPER WALL*

DIAGRAM 19 E

JUNIPER WALL

HIDDEN BUTTRESS

ACCESS

N

25 FEET

Exit Blues (diagram 20 E, route 1). Climber: Alex Andrews.
Belayer: Peter Cleveland. Photo: Sven Olof Swartling.

## JUNIPER WALL (Diagram 19 E)

ACCESS: See Diagram 18 E, West Terraces.

**13**  5.7. Short face route.
**14**  HIVE, 5.7. Corner.
**15**  5.4. Crack, 4 feet right of corner.
**16**  5.9. Climb face 3 feet right of route 15.
**17**  SQUIRM, 5.6. Inside corner, very awkward.
**18**  5.7. Face.
**19**  5.9. Right-slanting diagonal crack. Start climb as low as possible.
**20**  5.8. Start climb on lower wall, finish on corner above.
**21**  5.8. Crack in shallow V-depression.
**22**  5.8. Climb lower wall to high point.
**23**  5.6. Start in crack of lower wall, finish on face above.

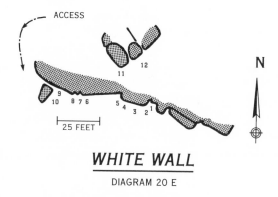

## WHITE WALL
DIAGRAM 20 E

## WHITE WALL (Diagram 20 E)

ACCESS: See Diagram 18 E, West Terraces.

**I**  EXIT BLUES, 5.11c. Climb corner and face left of gully. Move right to overhang, continue up face to crux near top.
**2**  SHORT PEOPLE NEED NOT APPLY, 5.12a. Start near corner or in deep crack and climb to overhang two-thirds of the way up. Move left to face with a long reach. Finish on face.
**3**  A MIDWESTERN CLIMB, 5.12a. Start 5 feet left of deep crack, climb center of White Wall. Finish right of

Purple Stripe (route 4), or on face as in Short People Need Not Apply (route 2).

**4** PURPLE STRIPE, 5.9. Start in crack below an obvious recess. Climb crack and recess to a 2-foot wide ledge. Move right a few feet and climb face and upper thin crack to top.

**5** 5.6. Start in crack and climb into recess, finish in upper inside corner left of overhanging nose.

**6** EASTER ISLAND, 5.7. Start on free-standing block and climb face, finish in short crack near top.

**7** 5.8. Climb inside corners, lower and upper, staying right of rib. Quite awkward stems at the start. Avoid use of rib on left.

**8** UNSATISFACTORILY, 5.6. Climb crack left of rib.

**9** BEHIND AKU, 5.4. Crack.

**10** AKU AKU, 5.7. Climb east face of tower; avoid using corners.

**11** 5.9. Corner and face of small tower.

**12** 5.7. Face of tower.

## POISON IVY WALL (Diagram 21 E)

ACCESS: See Diagram 18 E, West Terraces.

**1** LOST ARROW, 5.6. Climb northeast side of tower.

**2** RAMSES III, 5.7. Start climb on a face just right of crack, continue on south facing ramp. Finish by climbing overhang.

**3** UNDER THE BOTTLE, 5.11b. Climb face right of center. There is an obvious undercling at 15 feet. Do not use upper left corner.

**4** RAMSES II, 5.7. Crack system with overhang at top.

**5** RAMSES I, 5.7. Crack with overhang.

**6** RIGHT OF BLANKNESS, 5.8. Face near inside corner.

**7** BROKEN HOLD, 5.10a. Short face route.

**8** 5.6. Climb lowest face, finish on blocks at top.

**9** PORTRAIT CORNER, 5.8. Start just left of corner, at 10 feet move right to corner. Follow corner to top.

**10** SAY CHEESE, 5.10a. Climb center of face on small holds.

Under the Bottle (diagram 21 E, route 3). Climber: Peter Cleveland.
Photo: Alex Andrews.

Say Cheese (diagram 21 E, route 10). Climber: Keith Blackwell.
Photo: Sven Olof Swartling.

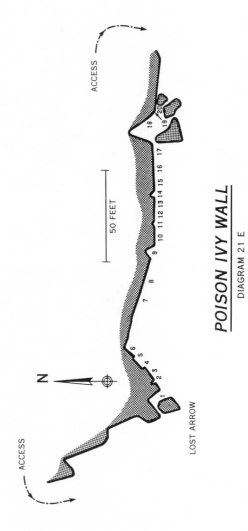

N

POISON IVY WALL

DIAGRAM 21 E

50 FEET

ACCESS

ACCESS

LOST ARROW

**11**  DECEPTION, 5.6. Left-leaning, wide crack.

**12**  5.5. Crack system.

**13**  5.8. Start in shallow V-crack near wide chimney (route 14), climb to ledge with block, finish on face above. Do not step on block.

**14**  5.5. Wide chimney crack.

**15**  WEEPING QUARTZ LEFT, 5.8. Climb face 4 to 5 feet right of route 14.

**16**  WEEPING QUARTZ RIGHT, 5.6. Climb left center of face.

**17**  5.7. Climb diagonally up just left of white quartz rock. Climbs 18 through 20 start from a platform 10 feet up.

**18**  SLUGGO, 5.6. Crack in southwest face.

**19**  PETE'S 10, 5.8. Corner. Climb, staying as close to corner as possible.

**20**  NANCY, 5.8. Face 4 feet right of corner.


## BIRD-FOOT BUTTRESS a.k.a. AMERICAN DREAM AREA (Diagram 22 E)

ACCESS: See Diagram 18 E, West Terraces.

**1**  BIRD SEED, 5.8. Overhanging wall and crack.

**2**  5.5. Chimney.

**3**  PAY OFF, 5.7. Face.

**4**  LITTLE BIRD, 5.8. Climb crack near southwest corner, staying on right side of corner.
*Variation*, 5.7. Climb on and left of corner.

**5**  SICK VULTURE, 5.8. Climb lower corner and upper face. Finish just right of center crack in overhang.
*Variation*, 5.10b. Start farther left; avoid right lower corner.

**6**  SQUEEZE PLAY, 5.8. Start in chimney, climb to overhang, move out and step right, continue to top. Very awkward.

**7**  PROCTO PETE AND THE ENDOS, 5.12b. Face just right of Squeeze Play (route 6).

**8**  MOTHER AND APPLE PIE, 5.9. Start in middle of face, climb diagonally up and right to thin crack near

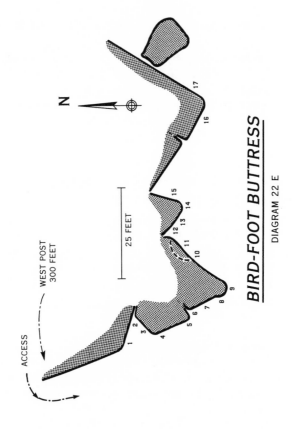

**N**

ACCESS

WEST POST
300 FEET

25 FEET

1 2
3
4
5 6
7
8
9
10
11
12
13
14
15
16
17

*BIRD-FOOT BUTTRESS*

DIAGRAM 22 E

corner. Follow crack to a surprise near top. Avoid using corner.

**9**  HARD NOSE, 5.8. Corner.

**10**  ELLIS ISLAND, 5.8. Start from block and climb up and right to top.

**11**  AMERICAN DREAM ROOF, 5.10d. Start above the lower overhang, climb the 5-foot overhang directly, using finger holds under the roof and large bucket holds above. *Variation,* AMERICAN DREAM DIRECT, 5.11a. Start on left side of lower overhang, move right and up.

**12**  5.5. Chimney.

**13**  5.7. Face just right of chimney.

**14**  DOVE TAIL LEFT, 5.7. Corner.

**15**  DOVE TAIL RIGHT, 5.6. Climb crack just right of corner.

**16**  5.7. Climb corner and move left near top.

**17**  5.7. Face.

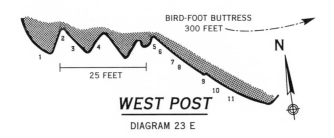

WEST POST

DIAGRAM 23 E

## WEST POST (Diagram 23 E)

West Post is a small outcropping well hidden in the forest, 300 feet west of Bird-Foot Buttress. All of the climbs are short.

**1**  THE POST, 5.8. Face route near corner.

**2**  R.C., 5.10c. Overhanging inside corner and crack.

**3**  OUTSIDE R.C., 5.10d. Start 6 feet right of R.C. (route 2), climb into hanging inside corner.

**4**  I SEE THE BUCKET, 5.10b. Climb face and left corner. *Variation,* 5.11a. Avoid using left corner.

**5**  ROTTEN ATTITUDE, 5.8. Inside corner.

**6**  5.7. Crack.

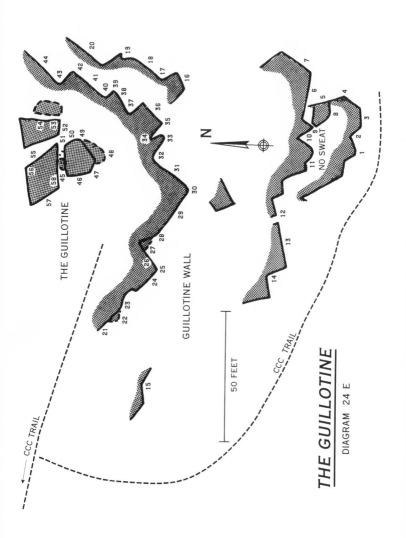

# THE GUILLOTINE

## DIAGRAM 24 E

100

**7** 5.9. Face crack. Avoid using route 6 crack and right corner.

**8** 5.4. Crack.

**9** 5.4. Inside corner.

**l0** 5.8. Crack leaning left.

**ll** 5.9. Double crack.

# The Guillotine (Diagram 24 E)

The first rock outcroppings along the CCC Trail, which starts .5 mile east of the south shore parking and picnic area, form a broken ridge on the upper bluff. The climbs are on three main levels: No Sweat, Guillotine Wall, and The Guillotine.

The Guillotine is a cluster of towers standing on the platform above Guillotine Wall. The name comes from a suggestive wedge-shaped chockstone between two of the towers. A considerable number and variety of short climbs (20 to 30 feet) are concentrated on the towers and wall below. This is a good area for beginners and larger groups.

ACCESS: Ascend the CCC Trail. The first outcropping, No Sweat, is above three switchbacks in the wooded lower bluff. The Guillotine is located 100 feet above (north of) No Sweat.

## NO SWEAT (Diagram 24 E)

**l** 5.4. Rib/crack. Ascend easy steps behind tree to west end of No Sweat roof, use crack above to take high step and climb to ledge. A good point to start ascent of the Guillotine ridge.

**2** NO SWEAT, 5.9. Climb strenuously through notch near center of roof.

**3** NO SWEAT OVERHANG, 5.11a a.k.a. THE BIRD, 5.11a. Start 5 feet right of No Sweat (route 2), dyno past very small 8-inch notch between nose of overhang and No Sweat.

**4** 5.8. Balance from right onto rock projecting from east end, step carefully high left above roof.
*Variation,* 5.9. Start from below and avoid projecting rock.

**5**   5.8. Hand traverse. Start left of chimney, traverse 6 feet left with handholds on a ledge, climb to ledge above.
*Variation*, 5.9. Climb straight up from bottom, avoiding hand traverse.

**6**   5.7. Climb wall right of easy chimney onto a mantleshelf, balance onto upper ledge, climb above or around right corner.

**7**   MONGO FURY, 5.10c. Climb cracks 3 feet right of corner.

**8–14**   A number of 15-foot climbs along the trail and above first ledge.

**15**   5.5. Traditional layback, a 15-foot sharp-edged crack along the trail. A faint path branches east at this point.

**16–20**   Minor wall with short climbs.


## GUILLOTINE WALL (Diagram 24 E)

**21**   5.7. Overhanging nose. Climb on left side.

**22**   5.9. Climb wall into inside corner, continue on nose above.

**23**   THE LITTLE THING, 5.1. Shallow chimney.

**24**   ANNIE'S OVERHANG, 5.7. Overhang/crack. Climb thin crack to overhang; using hand jam in left crack above overhang, climb right crack to top.

**25**   POISON IVY, 5.4. Corner, small holds at first.

**26**   RHUS TOXICODENDRON RADICANS, 5.8. Climb, staying right of corner.

**27**   LEVITATION, 5.5. A little levitation may help you to get off the ground (hardest part). Climb onto left side of slab, stem past first overhang, finish on left wall.
*Variation*, 5.9. Same start as Levitation. Continue on face left of Levitation.

**28**   LEVITATION, RIGHT SIDE, 5.6. Start at right side of slab and continue fairly straight up about 5 feet right of inside corner.
*Variation*, 5.11d. Start same as Levitation Right Side. At 8 feet, stretch far right and move up, avoiding holds on Labor Pains (route 29), finish straight up to top.

**29**   LABOR PAINS, 5.10b. Start at left limit of undercut section. The difficulty is concentrated in the first 6 feet.

**30**   5.7. Corner. Use a layback and pinch hold on right side to gain first corner ledge, continue up the corner onto next small ledge. A mantleshelf problem.

**31** BROKEN BOULDERS, 5.2. Crack starting from niche.
*Variation,* 5.2. Begin farther right on a slanting ledge.

**32** THE LAYBACK, 5.4. Layback, jamming left leg in the crack.
*Variation,* 5.7. Climb as a pure layback. Very strenuous.

**33** 5.5. Corner.

**34** BEGINNER'S CHIMNEY, 5.2. Chimney.

**35** BEGINNER'S NOSE, 5.2. Nose.

**36** BEGINNER'S FACE, 5.4. Climb 4 feet onto first ledge, then up left corner.
*Variation,* 5.6. Climb directly up middle and right side of face.

**37–44** East end of Guillotine Wall.

## THE GUILLOTINE (Diagram 24 E)

**45** GUILLOTINE WEST, 5.2. Chimney. Climb by bridging back and feet or by stemming. The latter method is neater.
*Variation,* 5.2. From upper chockstone traverse underneath top overhang on south tower.

**46** 5.4. Low level traverse 2 feet off ground.

**47** 5.7. Overhanging crack.

**48** 5.2. Ledges, easy except for retable at top.

**49** 5.3. Corner with small balance holds.

**50** BAREFOOT CRACK, 5.3. Face/cracks. A good climb to practice placing protection.

**51** GUILLOTINE EAST, 5.2. Chimney, easy stemming practice.

**52** 5.8. Narrow face with small holds.

**53** THE GOPHER, 5.7. Work up right side of corner onto small face holds, then grab for top.

**54** 5.7. Crack starting behind block.

**55** 5.2. Chimney.

**56** 5.4. Corner; climb straight up.

**57** ANARCHIST CRACK, 5.4. Crack leading to upper ledge.

**58** DECAPITATION, 5.7. Climb wall just right of corner to upper ledge, then climb on small holds to top.

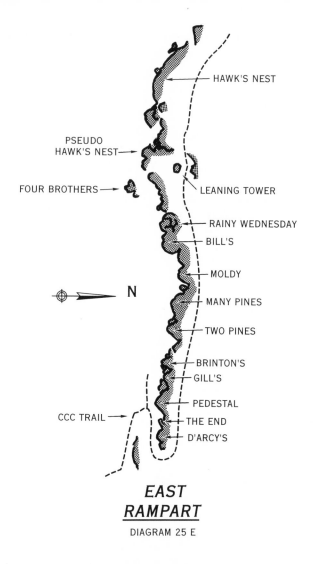

HAWK'S NEST

PSEUDO
HAWK'S NEST

FOUR BROTHERS

LEANING TOWER

RAINY WEDNESDAY

BILL'S

MOLDY

N

MANY PINES

TWO PINES

BRINTON'S

GILL'S

PEDESTAL

CCC TRAIL

THE END

D'ARCY'S

## *EAST RAMPART*

DIAGRAM 25 E

## East Rampart (Diagram 25 E)

This cliff band extends for .25 mile along the summit of the East Bluff and averages 80 feet in height. It is generally considered to have the finest climbing at Devil's Lake. Access is by the CCC Trail. After climbing past the first rock outcrop (No Sweat), the trail skirts a scenic boulderfield and turns abruptly left at the base of a short wall (The Monster). Just above, a climber's path splits off to the left (west) along the base of the rampart, while the trail continues up and right around the east end.

## THE MONSTER (Diagram 26 E)

**1**  THE FLATIRON, B1. This is a ghastly John Gill boulder problem (every area has them). Start on a smooth slab of rock 15 feet high, where the trail reaches the base of a subsidiary wall just below the summit cliff. Climb up the center of the slab. There are easier variations on the sides. *Variation,* B2. Climb using right crack only.

**2**  5.9. Start at top of The Flatiron (route 1) and climb the short wall above.

**3**  FRANKENSTEIN, 5.12b. Climb corner with small overhang.

**4**  THE MONSTER, 5.10c. A short, unfriendly crack. Start in a shallow alcove in the overhanging wall. Climb to top of alcove, continue in crack above.

**5**  THE THING, 5.7. A typical Devil's Lake paradox—how can it be so hard when it looks so easy? Start at base of chimney or groove (an approach from left or right is preferable to direct attack) and climb groove to top.

**6**  THE ZIPPER, B2. Tight seam just left of The Thing (route 5).

**7**  CLOSE TO THE THING, 5.8. Climb left corner of wall.

**8**  ALSO CLOSE TO THE THING, 5.8. Climb cracks in middle of face.

**9**  THE BODY SNATCHER, 5.7. Start below shallow chimney capped by an overhang. Climb crack at left to ledge at base of chimney, then up chimney, step left and up to top. It would be well not to fall traversing out from the chimney.

**10**  THE BODY SNATCHER DIRECT, 5.10c. Climb straight over overhang, avoiding holds on The Body Snatcher (route 9).

**11**  THE BODY SNATCHER VARIATION, 5.7. Start on

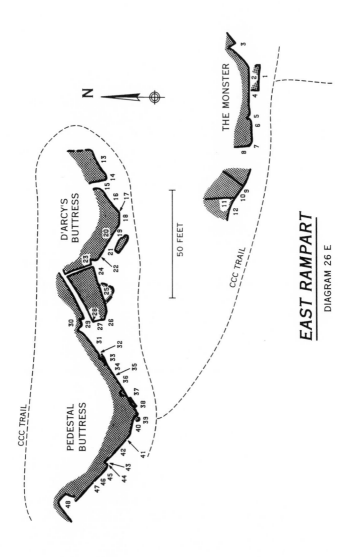

N

THE MONSTER

D'ARCY'S
BUTTRESS

PEDESTAL
BUTTRESS

CCC TRAIL

CCC TRAIL

50 FEET

## EAST RAMPART

DIAGRAM 26 E

bench just left of The Body Snatcher (route 9), climb flake and crack.

I2     THE CRAB, 5.9-B1. This is a short wall just left of The Body Snatcher (route 9); it can be climbed several different ways.

## D'ARCY'S BUTTRESS to PEDESTAL BUTTRESS (Diagram 26 E)

I3     CEMETERY WALL, 5.6. Short boulder problem. Start in center of face.

I4     SHIP'S PROW, 5.6. Jutting nose. Likened to keel-hauling.

I5     30 SECOND CRACK, 5.3. For those who are bothered by exposure.

I6     D'ARCY'S WALL, 5.8. Named for Ray D'Arcy, who never was able to make the last crux reach. Start on right side of wall near inside corner. Climb left to approximate center of wall, then up to top.

*Variation,* GRAND TRAVERSE, 5.8. From center of wall, traverse left around corner to Last Gasp (route 18).

I7     DEATH LEAP 2000, 5.10b a.k.a. BLOW YOUR NOSE, 5.10b. Start 8 feet right of corner, traverse left to corner, then move right onto large flakes of D'Arcy's Wall (route 16). Jump up and left for a bucket hold on Last Gasp (route 18). Finish on face right of corner.

*Variation,* PICK YOUR NOSE, 5.10d. Avoid bucket hold on Last Gasp (route 18).

I8     LAST GASP, 5.8. Many a climber has grasped the final ledge only to fall from utter exhaustion. Start in pit slightly left of corner (starting from adjacent rocks is strictly frowned upon). Struggle up to ledge, continue close to corner to top.

I9     EASY OVERHANG, 5.4. Offers an introductory course in the use of buckets. Climb to ledge behind large block, traverse to right crack, negotiate overhang, and continue to top.

20     STRAWBERRY FIELDS, 5.9. Climb bulge left of Easy Overhang (route 19), surmount overhang, then continue directly to top.

A climb to the left of Sometime Crack Right Side (diagram 26 E, route 24). Climber: Paul Wagener. Photo: Alex Andrews.

**21** ZIG-ZAG, 5.5. This line follows left crack behind the block. Climb to ledge behind large block, zig left and zag right to clear overhang, continue in crack to top. Try to be one of Devil's Lake's select few who don't use the Linden tree.

**22** 5.9. Climb corner left of Zig-Zag (route 21) to roof, continue over roof to top.

**23** DARKNESS AT NOON, 5.2. Stygian chimney.

**24** SOMETIME CRACK RIGHT SIDE, 5.10b/10c. Thin crack on right side of the overhanging wall. Climb crack to alcove, then up left to Sometime Crack (route 25).

**25** SOMETIME CRACK, 5.10a. When queried about whether they lead this climb, climbers typically give the evasive response "sometime." Start on slab 15 feet high at base of overhanging jam crack. Climb jam crack to intersection with horizontal crack, traverse 5 feet right, then up to top. NOTE: On top rope, watch for severe pendulum.

BLOW-UP, 5.10b. At horizontal crack, hand traverse left to corner, then up crack to top.

SOMETIME DIRECT, 5.10d. At horizontal crack, continue up center of wall past big bucket hold to top. Not topping out avoids the last hard mantle move.

WELFARE LINE, 5.12b. Climb overhanging face between Sometime Crack and Sometime Left.

SOMETIME LEFT, 5.11d. Start on platform, 6 feet left of crack, climb overhanging wall to horizontal crack. Traverse right and finish on Sometime Direct.

**26** BATMAN, 5.12a/12b. Start under The End (route 27) and traverse up and right around corner on good holds. Then traverse back left on thin holds to arete and follow arete to top.

**27** THE END, 5.10a. One's last lead at Devil's Lake? Start on block outside the deep cleft, traverse right onto the narrow overhanging wall, climb wall (if lucky) to top.

*Variation,* THE END DIRECT, 5.10b. Start on bottom, avoiding the block.

**28** END OF THE END, 5.10a. Start on same block as The End (route 27), climb corner above; i.e., left corner of The End.

**29**    CHIMNEY'S END, 5.4. Deep cleft behind The End (route 27). Can be ascended as a chimney.

**30**    THE BEGINNING, 5.7. Groove or V-chimney.

**31**    THE STRETCHER, 5.9+/10a. Start on smooth face 10 feet right of Birch Tree Crack (route 32). A couple of long reaches, then up, up, up to top.

*Variation*, 5.10b. Same start, but climb up and slightly left near Birch Tree Crack (route 32).

PETE'S LAMENT, 5.12b. Climb blank-looking face right of The Stretcher.

**32**    BIRCH TREE CRACK, 5.8. This is a one-move climb. Without the proper technique it becomes a no-move retreat. The birch tree that once grew here could not stand the continual abuse of falling climbers. Start on ledge 10 feet up, climb into alcove, then up crack to top.

**33**    HOURGLASS, 5.11c. Start from alcove of Birch Tree Crack (route 32), traverse left onto face, continue as in Hourglass Direct.

HOURGLASS DIRECT, 5.12a. Start from ledge 10 feet up, just left of Birch Tree Crack (route 32), and climb face straight to top.

**34**    UPPER DIAGONAL, 5.9. Start on same ledge as Birch Tree Crack (route 32). Climb left into diagonal crack and follow to top. Strenuous, can be well protected.

FLAKE ROUTE, 5.10d. Climb face left of Upper Diagonal to alcove with fixed pin. From alcove move right to the obvious flake, continue up and slightly right to top.

ANGLE OF DANGLE, 5.12a. From the flake climb to thin crack; at end of crack move left to face. Hard on the fingertips.

**35**    SWEATSHOP, 5.11b. Climb wall, staying between Upper and Lower Diagonal (routes 34 and 36).

**36**    LOWER DIAGONAL, 5.8. Offers experience in placing protection on the run. Start near base of large pine tree, up to (lower) diagonal crack, climb crack to ledge at left corner, exit left.

*Variation*, THE TRICK, 5.8. From ledge, finish by attacking wall directly, a bit left of corner.

**37**    THE PEDESTAL, 5.4. A traditional two-pitch climb. First pitch: start below detached flake, climb right edge to top of the flake (pedestal), traverse left (crux) around

Upper Diagonal (diagram 26 E, route 34). Climber: Lorene
Marcinek. Photo: Alex Andrews.

corner to hidden triangular belay ledge. Second pitch: traverse farther left to pine tree, climb crack to upper ledge, from which several finishes are possible.

**38** CONDOLENCES, 5.7. A straighter version of The Pedestal (route 37). Start under left edge of the flake. Climb crack and overhang, then up onto the flake (crux). Traverse left to corner, climb corner past bulges to ledge (same ledge as Lower Diagonal, route 36).

*Variation,* 5.11b. At 10 feet climb short face with sharp finger holds just left of The Pedestal (route 37) flake.

**39** GOLDEN LEDGES, 5.11b. The gold is fool's gold, as well as the ledges. Start just left of corner, climb into groove on the corner, then up to traverse on The Pedestal (route 37).

**40** ALL THE WAY, 5.12b. No easy moves on this climb. Start in groove 5 feet right of Congratulations (route 41), then straight up face to The Pedestal (route 37) belay ledge, continue straight up.

*Variation,* 5.11d. Start from left, avoiding the groove.

**41** CONGRATULATIONS, 5.10a. One of the classic "hard" routes, the scene of many falls. Climb the steep crack leading to pine tree.

**42** ASSUME THE POSITION, 5.12b. A thin face route left of Congratulations (route 41). The face is gained by a traverse from the left.

**43** RICH & FAMOUS, 5.11d. Start up Ironmongers (route 44) and climb to small pedestal. Traverse 6 feet right under overhang, then up bulging overhang to top. Do not use bucket hold on Pine Box (route 44 variation).

**44** IRONMONGERS, 5.7. Start at base of tree, climb into alcove, step left and up the crack to ledge.

*Variation,* PINE BOX, 5.10a. Climb straight up from alcove.

**45** IRONMONGERS SUPER DIRECT, 5.11a. Start 5 feet left of Ironmongers (route 44). Everything but the corner is legal.

**46** EVELYN BITES THE CRUST, 5.10b. Climb 12 inches to the left of Ironmongers Super Direct (route 45).

**47** LETHE, 5.7. Climb slabby wall past overhang to ledge. An easy crack leads to top.

**48** 5.2. Easy climbs in upper recess.

## GILL'S BUTTRESS to TWO PINES BUTTRESS (Diagram 27 E)

**49** FANTASY, 5.9. Start at base of smooth wall. Climb up 10 feet, then 8 feet right, then back left into notch at top of the wall.
*Variation,* WEASELS RIPPED MY FLESH, 5.12a. Climb straight up to upper notch.

**50** IN SEARCH OF THE LOST LIBIDO, 5.12b. Climb left of Fantasy (route 49).

**51** THE SPINE, 5.4. Deep groove or chimney. Start at crack on left side, climb into groove and up.
*Variation,* 5.6. Eliminate right wall of the groove.

**52** ACID ROCK, 5.12a. Smooth high wall left of The Spine (route 51). Start on top of large block, climb 5 feet on right side of wall. Traverse up and left to flake, then up and farther left to good ledge near left corner. Continue up and right, finishing in center of wall.
*Variation,* SLUT FOR PUNISHMENT, 5.12a. Same start, but climb straight to top. Very thin and complicated.

**53** PEYOTE BLUES, 5.12b. Start on block below Acid Rock (route 52), step across to wall. Traverse up and left to corner, follow corner to top.
*Variation,* ICE, 5.13a. Start in chimney right of Gill's Nose (route 54). Climb face with a series of very thin moves to meet Peyote Blues.

**54** GILL'S NOSE, 5.11b. Start at base of corner and climb face just left of corner.
*Variation,* 5.11c. At the top, climb on corner.

**55** GILL'S CHEEK, 5.11d/12a. Climb wall between Gill's Nose (route 54) and Gill's Crack (route 56), avoiding holds on other climbs.

**56** GILL'S CRACK, 5.10b/10c. Start halfway up slab in Boyscout (route 57), climb crack in right-hand wall. A John Gill on-sight solo.

**57** BOY SCOUT, 5.3. A standard "easy" route often crammed with beginners. Climb slab (many variations) to base of large chimney, then up chimney to top.

**58** RUBBER MAN, 5.13b. Start on pedestal right of Cheap Thrills (route 59). The first move is a very hard mantle.

**59** CHEAP THRILLS, 5.12b/12c. Start at left top edge of

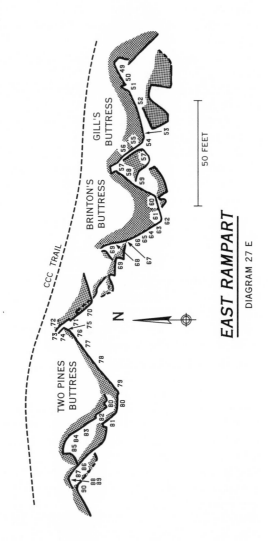

## EAST RAMPART

DIAGRAM 27 E

50 FEET

N

CCC TRAIL

TWO PINES BUTTRESS

BRINTON'S BUTTRESS

GILL'S BUTTRESS

slab in Boyscout (route 57). Climb to top, staying right of the corner.

**60** CHIAROSCURO, 5.9+. Start at semi-corner 10 feet right of Brinton's Crack (route 61), directly below Hilton Ledge (see Brinton's Crack description). Climb face left of corner to Hilton Ledge, then directly up wall to top.

*Variation,* 5.9. Start from left side of slab in Boyscout (route 57), climb thin crack to Hilton Ledge.

**61** BRINTON'S CRACK, 5.6. A classic climb made worthwhile by a continuous series of exposed moves. It was first ascended in 1941; its crux still embarrasses many climbers. Scramble 20 feet up slabby rock to crack near corner of the buttress. Climb crack to just below rectangular niche, traverse delicately right to (or almost to) a platform (Hilton Ledge), then up jam crack to top.

*Variation,* BRINTON'S DIRECT, 5.8. From rectangular niche, climb near corner to top.

**62** BRINTON'S CORNER, 5.10a. Climb corner all the way to top.

**63** ROCOCO VARIATIONS, 5.7. Start near right corner, climb flake crack 30 feet to join Berkeley (route 64).

*Variation,* STOOL PIDGEON, 5.11b. At end of flake crack, continue straight up wall.

**64** BERKELEY, 5.6. Another classic. Start at crack 20 feet left of buttress corner. Climb crack 20 feet, then traverse right to ledge under first small overhang. Move up right, then climb somewhat left to exit crack leading into hanging chimney. This route can be varied considerably.

**65** SOUTHSIDE, 5.12a. Climb through small overhang 5 feet right of niche; avoid the holds on Berkeley (route 64) and Chicago (route 66).

**66** CHICAGO, 5.8. One of the earlier "hero" climbs. The quality of the protection is poor. Start in same crack as Berkeley (route 64). Climb 25 feet to triangular niche (last protection until after crux), continue up the crack past long sustained crux, surmount final overhang just below top.

**67** EVANSTON TOWNSHIP, 5.10b. Start from platform at base of Puff N' Grunt Chimney (route 69), climb thin crack parallel to Chicago (route 66).

*Variation,* 5.11b. Climb lower wall without using rock on the left.

**68**   GOLF ROAD, 5.10d. Start on platform, climb face right of chimney.

**69**   PUFF N' GRUNT CHIMNEY, 5.6. Climb one of two inside corners to base of the chimney, then up chimney to top. Several wedged chockstones are useful.

**70**   THE RACK, 5.7. Start at crack curving right, capped by overhang. Follow crack to small platform on right corner, step up left (crux) and climb corner blocks to ledge. Finish on wall right of the corner.

*Variation,* 5.6. From small platform on right corner traverse right 10 feet and climb wall to corner blocks.

**71**   THOROUGHFARE, 5.11a. Start 5 feet right of The Grotto (route 73), climb inside corner with use of adjacent (right) crack. Continue up thin cracks on the spectacular green wall above.

CROSS TOWN TRAFFIC, 5.11d/12a. Start 4 to 5 feet right of Thoroughfare. Climb up and left to a solution pocket, continue using only the right-hand crack. A difficult start leading to arm-burning finish.

L.S.D., 5.11c. Climb using only left crack of Thoroughfare.

**72**   LUNAR ECLIPSE, 5.11a. Climb crack in right wall of The Grotto (route 73). Continue up, through the middle of the higher, right overhang. When falling, watch your back.

**73**   THE GROTTO, 5.4. Start in dark chimney, climb past chockstones to platform on outside (top of chimney is filled with rock). Finish using crack or inside corner above the platform.

**74**   SOLAR ECLIPSE, 5.7. Climb left wall 4 feet inside The Grotto (route 73).

**75**   MOUSE TRAP, 5.11d. Climb narrow face near corner right of Vacillation (route 76).

**76**   VACILLATION, 5.7. Climb crack with bulge 10 feet up. Two-thirds of the way up, move right to wide crack to top.

**77**   MOUSE'S MISERY, 5.10a. Face just left of Vacillation (route 76). Climb 25 feet up and left to overhang, turn overhang at left crack, and follow crack to top.

MOUSE TRACKS, 5.11a. Climb right side of overhang, continue by using a heel hook into the appalling-looking solution pockets above.

MOUSE'S TAIL, 5.11c. Climb Mouse's Misery to triangular roof on right, traverse right and up arch. Continue up between Mouse Tracks and Vacillation (route 76). Avoid the temptation of good holds on Vacillation.

**78** FULL STOP, 5.6. Another classic, originally called "Two Pines." Climb thin crack leading to square niche. From the niche climb over elephant ear bulge, move 5 feet left and up to hanging gully with several pine trees. NOTE: There may be loose rock on ledge. Traverse right onto broken section of the wall and continue to top.

BIG DEAL, 5.10a. Above elephant ear bulge, climb thin crack about 5 feet left of Mouse's Misery (route 77).

**79** REPRIEVE, 5.7. Start just right of corner, climb up (crux not high off ground) and left to a stance. Continue up face, staying right of the corner.

**80** SCHIZOPHRENIA, 5.6. Start below overhanging nose 25 feet up. Climb into dark pocket, continue around left side of nose (or directly over it), then up ridge above.

**8I** MODERATION, 5.4. Start up broken rock, traverse right above nose on Schizophrenia (route 80), then up the easy ridge.

*Variation,* 5.5. Start the same, but continue straight up groove that intersects the ridge higher up, rather than climb ridge.

**82** BROTHER WITHOUT A BRAIN, 5.11a. Start part way up Moderation (route 81), climb overhang and outside corner.

A rock and clay gully (5.2) angles steeply left from the start of Moderation (route 81). It provides access to the next three climbs or the top.

**83** TOUCH AND GO, 5.7. Start halfway up the gully, at base of steep wall. Move up right, then back left, following a set of small ledges to top of the crackless green wall.

**84** DYSPEPSIA, 5.6. About halfway up this wall you'll wish for your pills. Start in same gully as Touch and Go (route 83). Climb crack on left side of the steep wall, ending just right of the dark overhang near top.

PUSSY GALORE'S FLYING CIRCUS, 5.7. Start below flake (detached block) in line with the dark overhang.

Climb edge of the flake and continue until below right side of overhang. Instead of exiting right, traverse left on good footholds, then up (crux) to top.

**85**  JOLLY GENDARME, 5.4. Start in upper part of the gully, traverse left around the gendarme (on southwest side of the gully) to crack with pine tree, climb crack.

**86**  GERITOL, 5.11c. Start at base of wall with dirty yellow lichen. Climb on the very small awkward holds until below hanging corner, then up right side of corner.

**87**  The wall between Geritol (route 86) and Chlorosis (route 88) has two cracks. Right crack, 5.10a. Left crack, 5.10d.

The following three climbs start in same inside corner.

**88**  CHLOROSIS, 5.7. Climb inside corner to overhang 30 feet up. Step right and climb overhang to crack above, follow crack to top.

**89**  HYPOGLYCEMIA, 5.7. Start from same inside corner as Chlorosis. Above the overhang, climb the overhanging crack and groove on right wall.

## MANY PINES BUTTRESS to BILL'S BUTTRESS (Diagram 28 E)

**90**  ANEMIA, 5.2. Originally called Many Pines. Start in same inside corner as Chlorosis (route 88) and Hypoglycemia (route 89), climb to ledge with first pine tree. Continue by one of several variations.

**91**  BROKEN LADDER, 5.7. Climb face up to the pine tree ledge. Continue by one of several variations.

**92**  PETER'S PROJECT RIGHT SIDE, 5.9. Climb the face about 5 feet right of Peter's Project (route 93). The crack is off limits.

**93**  PETER'S PROJECT, 5.7. Start in overhanging crack, climb crack until the angle eases, then move fairly straight up face and cracks to top.

**94**  OSTENTATION, 5.10a. Start just right of corner with overhang 10 feet up. Climb to overhang and traverse left around corner, then up right to the good holds. Continue on corner to top.

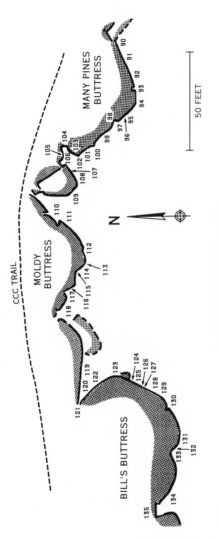

MANY PINES BUTTRESS

MOLDY BUTTRESS

BILL'S BUTTRESS

CCC TRAIL

N

50 FEET

*EAST RAMPART*

DIAGRAM 28 E

**95** CALLIPIGEANOUS CRACK, 5.10a. An exercise in muscular laybacking. Climb (finger) jam crack, then exit right to corner.

*Variation*, CALLIPIGEANOUS DIRECT, 5.11b. From jam crack continue straight up. Avoid use of good right-hand holds.

**96** ASLEEP IN A FUKNES DREAM, 5.12a a.k.a. THE INDIAN, 5.12a. This climb goes up between Callipigeanous Crack (route 95) and No Trump (route 97) all the way to the top.

**97** NO TRUMP, 5.11d. Start 3 feet right of Michael's Project (route 98) and stay within a few feet of the crack all the way to the top. Avoid holds in the crack.

**98** MICHAEL'S PROJECT, 5.7. Start in prominent groove and crack, 10–15 feet up step right to easier holds, then back into the crack until below overhang. Exit right to large ledge, from which there are a couple of ways to finish.

KAMA-KAZI, 5.8. Climb worming your way up inside corner crack. Finish directly up overhang to top.

**99** FLATUS, 5.11b. Easily identified by the lack of identifiable holds. Start below Black Rib (route 100), climb up and right past three bolts approximately 20 feet up, continue left under overhang and up.

*Variation*, FLATUS DIRECT, 5.11d. Do not traverse left under overhang, climb straight up to top.

*Variation*, FLATUS TRIPLE DIRECT, 5.11d. Another hard start. Start climb directly below bolts and climb straight to top.

**100** BLACK RIB, 5.11a. Getting off the ground is the first crux. Start in pit below dark section of the wall, climb to hanging chimney above.

**101** DOUBLE CLUTCH, 5.12a a.k.a. CHICKEN'S DON'T FLY, 5.12a. Climb face between Black Rib (route 100) and Man and Superman (route 102), over bulge to top.

**102** MAN AND SUPERMAN, 5.10d. Climb corner, finishing left at top.

**103** SUPERMAN, 5.12a. Face left of Man and Superman (route 102).

**104** SEWING MACHINE, 5.6. An unusual climb for Devil's Lake. One's legs give out before one's arms, unless legs

Double Clutch (diagram 28 E, route 101). Climber: Saul Sepsenwol.
Photo: Jim Horst.

and arms give out together. Climb dirty flaring chimney to top. Loose rock near top.

**105**  5.9. Climb face, starting from ledge part way up Sewing Machine (route 104).

**106**  JAMBOREE, 5.6. Start in chimney (which gives a 5.2 access route behind the small tower), then jam up deep cracks on right wall.

ALGAE, 5.4. Start left of chimney, follow a crack up and right to flake in the chimney.

*Variation,* 5.9. From top of crack climb left and up.

**107**  V8, 5.11a. Start up in center of wall until a move right leads to a high step, layback to top.

**108**  PLEASURES OF THE GROIN, 5.12b. Climb left side of tower, using same start as V8 (route 107), follow a straighter line, just to left of V8.

**109**  5.4. Climb the tower, starting near south corner.

**110**  LICHEN, 5.2. Climb behind one of the large flakes and continue up wall to top.

**111**  FUNGUS, 5.7. Climb face left of the flakes, using crusty holds.

**112**  NINE-MINUS, 5.8. Start in shallow inside corner capped by overhang. Climb up, exit right below overhang, then up and left.

TEN-MINUS, 5.10a. Climb the face right of inside corner, then left as in Nine-Minus.

ELEVEN-MINUS, 5.10d. Same start as Ten-Minus, continue directly up the face.

**113**  HALES CORNER, 5.10d. Start right of corner, move up and left to corner.

**114**  MOTHER OF PEARL, 5.10c. Climb face only, on right side of inside corner.

**115**  CUL-DE-SAC, 5.8. A deceptive line, it is much harder than it looks. Start in inside corner capped by square overhang. Climb up and right (crux) past the overhang. Scramble up short chimney to a ledge and to top.

*Variation,* CUL-DE-SAC EXIT, 5.11d. Mantle at roof, and continue, following corner to top.

**116**  FIBULA CRACKS, 5.12a/12b. Start in shallow inside corner 5 feet left of Cul-De-Sac (route 115). Climb straight up 35 feet and pass overhang on the right.

**117**  TIBIA CRACK, 5.8. Start in crack leading to hanging chimney between two overhangs. Climb crack, enter the chimney, and exit right.

**118** HORTICULTURE, 5.4. There are large rotten overhangs high up on this line. The most interesting start is on the outside of a semi-attached pillar. Climb pillar, then inside corner beneath the overhangs; exit right to top.
*Variation,* ROOFUS, 5.8. Exit left from the overhangs.

**119** DOG LEG, 5.4. Start in dirt gully near base of The Dark Corner (route 121). Climb groove that first angles right, then goes straight up. Continue on ledges to top.

**120** PROPHET'S HONOR, 5.9. Start in gully as above, climb overhanging wall to right of The Dark Corner (route 121).

**121** THE DARK CORNER, 5.4. A dark, stygian chimney.

**122** BREAKFAST OF CHAMPIONS, 5.8. Climb long jam crack ending on huge flake, then up left to top.

**123** IGNOMINY, 5.4. Start near corner, climb broken crack up and right onto northeast wall of the buttress (white rock), then up wall 10 feet. Continue up ledges into inside corner with pine tree, then to top.

**124** TIGER, 5.12a. Face just right of Cheatah (route 125). Bucket hold on right is out of bounds.

**125** CHEATAH, 5.10b. An exceptionally continuous route. Climb long crack which ends with a difficult layback (crux) near right corner.

NOTE: The following two climbs cross part way up.

**126** PUSSY CAT, 5.11a. Climb face left of Cheatah (route 125), using flake at start of climb, pull small overhang, then move left. Continue up right of Push-Mi, Pull-Yu (route 128) to top.

**127** TOM CAT, 5.12a. A very difficult start just left of Pussy Cat (route 126); climb arch, staying 4 feet left of crack.

**128** PUSH-MI, PULL-YU, 5.6. An old classic originally called Three Pines. A popular lead with excellent protection. Climb (several ways) to crack beginning 20 feet up with pine tree above, climb crack to the pine, then scramble up ledges to top.

**129** TALK TO THE ANIMALS, 5.10a. Climb face left of Push-Mi, Pull-Yu (route 128).

Cheatah (diagram 28 E, route 125). Climber: Jim Bater. Photo: Alex Andrews.

**130** AGNOSTIC, 5.7. Climb into prominent alcove, step left onto ledge, then climb face and thin crack directly above the alcove, passing left of pine tree.

**131** GRAND INQUISITOR, 5.7. An indistinct line that prohibits traversing to the easier climbs on either side. Start at lowest point of Bill's Buttress. Climb 10 feet to ledge, then up (slightly left) 15 feet into shallow groove or trough (obscure from the ground). Continue on easier rock to overhanging layback crack, up crack, ending on small tower.

**132** MR BUNNEY MEETS THE POULTRY MAN, 5.11a. Climb face right of Coatimundi Crack (route 133). Finish by climbing overhang at top.

**133** COATIMUNDI CRACK, 5.6. Climb prominent groove and crack past overhanging section and step right onto ledge, then up to base of corner with small tower above. Continue up near the corner or step left to ledge and stem up inside corner (V-chimney), ending behind the tower.
*Variation,* 5.10a. Finger crack on small tower.
OVEREXTENSION, 5.6. Exit left from the groove, angling up to first ledge on Escalation (route 134).

**134** ESCALATION, 5.6. Climb crack 20 feet to ledge and pine tree, then to another ledge and pine tree, and to top.
*Variation,* 5.6. From first ledge traverse right on a narrow exposed ledge, join either of the two preceding routes.
*Variation,* 5.9. From left side of first ledge, climb narrow southwest face, finishing on lichen-covered narrow buttress.

**135** THE OUTHOUSE, 5.7. Start under overhang between the two buttresses. Climb either side of both overhangs. The second overhang is a huge wedged block. An ugly climb.

## RAINY WEDNESDAY TOWER to LEANING TOWER GULLY (Diagram 29 E)

**136** 5.10b. Climb corner in gully behind upper section of Rainy Wednesday Tower.

**137** FALSE ALARM JAM, 5.6. The southeast side of Rainy Wednesday Tower. Start on broken rock, climb to obvious

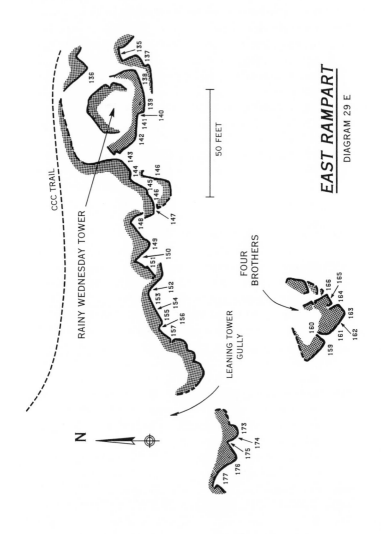

## EAST RAMPART

DIAGRAM 29 E

crack in red rock, climb crack to ledge, climb up either side of a slab boulder, continue on southeast face to top of the tower. Descent route: Climb down short chimney on northeast side and jump off behind the tower. Continue down chimney west of the tower to base of cliff.

**138** RESURRECTION, 5.10a. Start on a large block at base of smooth face (pointed ceiling above). Climb face near right edge until able to move left and up into bowl-shaped area. Continue up to ceiling and exit right.

*Variation*, 5.11d/12a. Climb up center of the smooth face, step left and up into bowl as above.

RESURRECTION RIGHT, 5.11c/11d. Climb face right of Resurrection.

**139** LAUNDRY CHUTE, 5.12a. Climb left side of face past two smaller overhangs, continue up and under right side of large overhang. Climb hanging chute in overhang.

NO STARCH, 5.11b/11c. Avoid chute, pass overhang on right.

**140** EAVE OF DESTRUCTION, 5.9+. Same start as Double Overhang (route 141) when under the ceiling, step right and up.

*Variation*, 5.7. Step right about 15 feet below the ceiling, then up corner.

**141** DOUBLE OVERHANG, 5.4. A well-protected route sufficiently exposed to maintain interest. Start in inside corner below ceiling, climb crack in corner, exit left and up to platform. Climb right onto "lemon squeezer" block then up into recess beneath right side of upper overhang. (If you climb directly up from the platform toward the overhang it is necessary to step right around a rib to attain this recess.) Step left and up into notch in the overhang, continue to top of the tower.

*Variation*, 5.7. At "lemon squeezer" traverse right 10 feet and step around corner into groove and climb to top.

**142** 5.4. Climb face directly to the platform.

**143** OUT OF THE WOODS, 5.8. Climb southeast face.

**144** BIRNAM WOOD, 5.7. Climb crack hidden, and jealousy guarded, by a tree.

**145** NEW LIGHT WAVES, 5.12b. Cracks and overhang right of Green Bulge (route 146). Climb slabs to first crack

(25 feet up), move left to pass overhang, move back right and follow thin cracks to top.

**146** GREEN BULGE, 5.7. Start at prominent red slab. Climb slab (various routes) to base of green bulge, up bulge (from left or right) to a ledge, continue up (crux shortly above the ledge), finish on small tower.

**147** MISS PIGGY'S PLEASURE, 5.8. Wall and short tower left of Green Bulge (route 146).

**148** THE BALCONY, 5.4. Climb the inside corner past a band of fairly unconsolidated rock.

**149** THE MEZZANINE, 5.4. Start on outside of minor buttress that reaches halfway up the wall. Climb the buttress to base of groove, climb groove to top.

**150** SECOND BALCONY, 5.4. Another inside corner or chimney. Climb the inside corner past a band of fairly unconsolidated rock.

**151** HIRSUTE, 5.7. Climb face and two overhangs.

**152** CEREBRATION, 5.4. Inside corner with overhang near top; pass overhang on right.
*Variation,* 5.4. Start at short jam crack to right of inside corner, then up broken rock.

**153** RESOLUTION, 5.9. Start 4 feet left of Cerebration (route 152). Climb straight up and join Second Coming (route 154) at 20-foot ledge.

**154** SECOND COMING, 5.7. Start at base of steep face. Climb layback "crack" 20 feet to ledge on right, continue up until it is possible to traverse left and up to top.
*Variation,* 5.8. Instead of traversing, continue straight up to top.

**155** ORGASM DIRECT, 5.11b. Climb 4 feet right of corner.

**156** ORGASM, 5.8. Try not to become overly excited by this intimidating line. Climb inside corner below large ceiling, continue up to smooth wall, mantle up, step right around corner and on to top.

**157** FOREPLAY, 5.6. Climb crack to pine tree, step right into inside corner left of the ceiling on Orgasm (route 156), then up past overhang to top. Watch for loose rock on top.

**158** THE FRICTION SLAB (not on diagram) is one of several boulder problems below Orgasm (route 156).

## FOUR BROTHERS (Diagram 29 E)

**159** FAMILY JEWELS, 5.7. Start from pedestal left of corner, step right around corner to hidden dihedral, climb dihedral. Finish in jam crack.

THE MIC, 5.11a. Same start as Family Jewels. At 10 feet move right and up overhang, face, and arete to top.

**160** GRAVEL PIT, 5.4. Climb the inside corner, laybacking past overhang into the gravel.

**161** MARY'S FACE, 5.9. Face left of Foliage (route 162).

**162** FOLIAGE, 5.4. Follow crack up and left across face.

**163** ZOT, 5.9. Start below corner overhang, and climb corner to top.

*Variation,* 5.7. Start at same crack as Foliage (route 162), step onto right corner, then climb corner to top.

**164** CATALEPSY, 5.6. Start in crack and climb into prominent groove above.

**165** 5.9. Climb face and up over small roof.

**166** DECADENCE, 5.4. Follow this grungy crack up to overhanging block, exit left when your belayer isn't looking.

## LEANING TOWER (Diagram 30 E)

**167** SOUTH FACE, 5.2. Climb center or either corner of face.

**168** WEST FACE, 5.8. Start from the right edge, climb the smooth face without using prominent holds (specifically the triangular niche) on left.

*Variation,* 5.2. Start at left corner (above low platform), climb up and right to top.

**169** NORTHWEST FACE, 5.7. Start in center of narrow face, climb up and right.

**170** NORTH FACE, 5.11a. Start at center of the smooth overhanging face, dyno to ledge, continue up to small pocket, up left to another pocket, then to top.

*Variation,* COSMIC CRINGE, 5.11b. Direct start.

**171** EAST FACE, 5.7. Start at right edge, climb up and left to top of overhanging wall.

*Variation,* 5.7. Start at left edge of face.

**172** THE TOMBSTONE is the short wall across the trail from

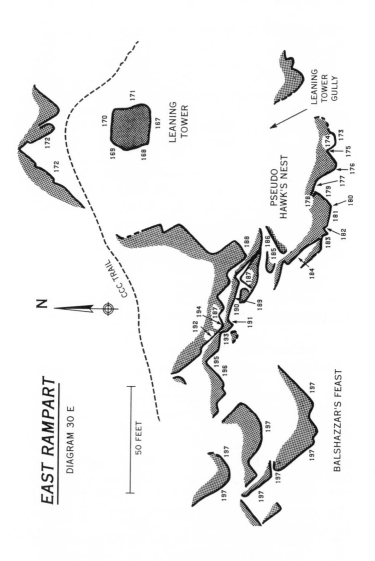

## EAST RAMPART

DIAGRAM 30 E

N

50 FEET

CCC TRAIL

LEANING TOWER

LEANING TOWER GULLY

PSEUDO HAWK'S NEST

BALSHAZZAR'S FEAST

Leaning Tower. Many variations are possible, some very difficult.

## PSEUDO HAWK'S NEST to BALSHAZZAR'S FEAST (Diagram 30 E)

**173** WILD HORSES, 5.8. Start at corner below right side of overhanging nose. Climb until above overhang, then up slab or left corner. Erosion and rock breakage keep making this climb harder.

**174** IMMACULATE CONCEPTION, 5.10a. Steep narrow wall just right of The Pretzel (route 175). Climb face only, to top.

**175** THE PRETZEL, 5.6. Is the name of this climb also a description of the climber on it? Start in the inside corner, which is very steep for 15 feet, then follow crack to top.

**176** DRUNKEN SAILOR, 5.5. Many climbers lose their bearings on this route. Start left of nose, move up and right 15 feet to a stance, then wander up the broad rounded ridge to top.

**177** EPIPHANY, 5.9. Climb crack in face to right of inside corner, eliminating wall to the left.

**178** CRACKING UP, 5.6. Prominent inside corner and crack with the crux at top.

**179** BAGATELLE, 5.12c/12d. Climb mini-overhang to crack, up left of crack to temporary rest stance at 20 feet. From stance move right and climb zigzagging up to, and past, an 8-inch overhang at 35 feet. Climb center of face to top.

PHLOGISTON, 5.12d. Left crack in same wall. Avoid use of left corner. A contrived but excellent climb.

**180** BEGINNER'S DEMISE, 5.11a. Start at base of steep wall just left of corner, climb wall near or on corner to easier rock above. Difficult bulge can be passed by a few unusual moves.

**181** ABM, 5.11a/11b. Often mistaken for Beginner's Demise (route 180). The route runs 4 to 6 feet left of Beginner's Demise. Start on short difficult wall and continue up over easier rock.

**182** CHICKEN DELIGHT, 5.7. Start just right of sharp narrow rib, climb layback crack 15 feet, continue straight up past overhanging block at 35 feet, then to top.

CHICKEN TONIGHT, 5.8. Stay left of Chicken Delight, climb steep hard crack.

**183** BEGINNER'S DELIGHT, 5.4. An aptly named climb. Several variations are possible at the start. Climb 30 feet to detached block, traverse right to corner or climb crack to below overhanging block, then traverse, climb corner to top.

FULL MOON OVER BARABOO, 5.9. Climb wall and roof above the start of Beginner's Delight.

**184** HERO'S FRIGHT, 5.7. Climb lower wall to base of the crack visible near upper left corner, follow crack to top.

**185** COUCH OF PAIN, 5.12a. Climb center of wall on small holds to top.

**186** SOFA-ISTICATED-LADY, 5.10d. Climb on left side of wall through small niche.

**187** DEATH AND TRANSFIGURATION, 5.4. Climb (any way) onto large narrow blocks detached from the wall, step into prominent dihedral, climb past black bulge of loose rock to a broad ledge. Walk off right or climb to top in crack 20 feet left.

*Variation*, 5.8. Start on right block (near auxiliary access gully), climb bulging wall above.

**188** FALLEN BIRCH, 5.5. Climb cracks and overhang.

**189** DEATH AND DISFIGURATION, 5.8. Start on left detached block, climb thin crack to broad ledge.

**190** DEGRADE MY SISTER, 5.11a. Face right of Prime Rib (route 191). Start from block, climb up and right, then left to obvious undercling. Finish 5 to 6 feet left of tree.

*Variation*, 5.12a. Direct start; climb face just right of inside corner.

**191** PRIME RIB, 5.9+. Ascend the rib until it fades at the level of the overhang on Bloody Mary (route 193), then up slightly left past small niche to the broad ledge.

*Variation*, 5.11d. Direct start.

*Variation*, 5.9. Climb right of rib, using a series of laybacks.

**192** 5.11b. Face on the upper level above Bloody Mary (route 193).

Bagatelle (diagram 30 E, route 179). Climber: Mike von Wahlde.
Photo: Fred Keesy.

**193** BLOODY MARY, 5.8. Look for large bulge of loose rock with a meaty crack through the center. Start in groove directly below the bulge, climb the groove, surmount the overhang by hand jams and face holds to an awkward stance, then up left to ledge left of prominent upper corner. Finish on wall above the ledge.

*Variation,* THE FAKIR, 5.7. Start at same point, climb left crack 20 feet to a platform, traverse up and right to the awkward stance.

**194** THARSIS, 5.11c. Start on upper ledge, climb crack right of corner, then move left to corner, follow corner to top.

**195** OCTOBER FIRST, 5.7. Inside corner, a strenuous layback that degenerates after the first few moves.

**196** ANCHOR'S AWAY, 5.6–5.8. Steep short wall with two cracks. Climb cracks behind either pine tree. (Left crack is 5.6.)

**197** BALSHAZZAR'S FEAST, 5.4–5.7. A veritable feast of climbing, in three courses. There are many variations, especially on the lowest wall.

## HAWK'S NEST (Diagram 31 E)

**198** R. EXAM, 5.9. Climb, following black water marks; pass small 8-inch overhang on right.

**199** HAPPY HUNTING GROUNDS, 5.11a. Climb thin steep crack, continue to ceiling high on the wall, climb out over right side to top. Leaders who fall on this climb may go the Happy Hunting Grounds.

**200** FLAKES AWAY, 5.11d/12a. Climb wall 4 to 5 feet left of Happy Hunting Grounds (route 199).

**201** DOUBLE HERNIA, 5.12a. Climb, following thin crack to ledge at 20 feet. Continue right of corner; do not use corner.

**202** BUCKET BRIGADE, 5.6. Start in The Funnel, a cleft or groove 25 feet high, climb to broken rock and bushes, where two main variations branch out. Bucket Brigade is the more easterly alternative. Continue almost straight up for 30 feet to ledge at base of prominent inside corner. Climb the inside corner past overhang to top.

*Variation,* HALLUCINATION, 5.4. At 30-foot ledge,

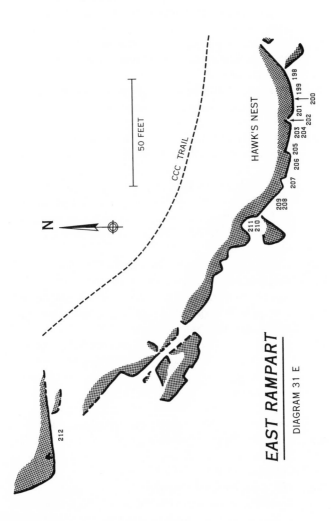

N

50 FEET

CCC TRAIL

HAWK'S NEST

212

211
210

209
208

207

206 205

204
203
202
201 199 198
200

*EAST RAMPART*

DIAGRAM 31 E

step right to outside ledge, then up and left to exit crack in wall above.

*Variation,* THE RAMP, 5.6. From top of The Funnel climb left wall 15 feet to base of lower angle slab. Climb either side of the slab, then up to broad ledge. The ledge system west of this point is commonly used to traverse off the wall. Climb the obvious chimney at the east end of the ledge or climb the wall at one of several points west of the chimney.

*Variation,* WALPURGISNACHT, 5.6. From broad ledge traverse right and enter a hanging groove, climb groove to top.

**203** NO FRUIT PLEASE, 5.11b. Start climb just left of The Funnel in Bucket Brigade (route 202) and climb face straight to top.

**204** PIEPLATE, 5.11a/11b. Same start as No Fruit Please (route 203). Climb up and left a few feet on pieplate holds, then straight to top.

*Variation,* 5.11a/11b. Direct start that begins with a lunge.

**205** VIVISECTION, 5.11a. This climb has an unforgettable start, particularly if you lose your fingers on it. Start beneath overhang 5 feet off the ground. Conquer overhang onto small slab, pass smaller overhang, then climb straight up cracks to top.

**206** ALPHA CENTAURI, 5.10d. Start a few feet left of Vivisection (route 205) on a slightly overhanging, disjointed crack and layback system. Climb 10 feet (crux), continue up the steep ledges as in Vivisection.

YELLOW PAGES, 5.11a. Start from top of block. Let your fingrs do the walking and join Alpha Centauri at 12 feet. Use care at start when top roping.

**207** ANOMIE, 5.8. Climb into alcove 15 feet off the ground. Climb out to the right, follow a shallow trough or concavity that angles slightly right.

*Variation,* MOTHER FLETCHER'S, 5.8. From the alcove climb up left to join Charybdis (route 208). There is no easy way out from this alcove.

**208** CHARYBDIS, 5.7. A magnificent line. The climbing is very continuous, but well protected. Start 15 feet right of inside corner formed by a large block. Climb 15 feet straight up, then follow thin crack angling slightly right, continue up to the exit ledge and top.

Left of Charybdis is a red boulder with a small roof at 15 feet with two climbs.

> RUDY'S B2, 5.9. Climb face. The left edge and crack are illegal.
> RUDY'S BROTHER, 5.10a. Climb just behind the tree.

**209** SCYLLA, 5.7. Climb 15 feet as in Charybdis (route 208), then continue slightly left to a comfortable ledge 30 feet up. Climb into dark overhang or dihedral that rises steeply to the right, follow it to highest overhanging point or step right from ledge and climb face to same point, then to top.

**210** CORONARY, 5.7. Start on the large block at west end of the wall. You can walk or climb up to this point. Move up and right, mantling onto a ledge (same as on Scylla, route 209). Step left and up to a possibly loose block between two prominent overhangs, then up the shallow right groove. There is a left groove accessible by stepping left from the loose block.
*Variation,* ANGINA, 5.9. Start on same block, climb up toward the overhang above, exit right and directly up into left groove of Coronary.

**211** ANGINA II, 5.9. Climb past Angina overhang, on left, into hanging inside corner.

**212** LAND'S END, 5.7. The rock immediately west of Hawk's Nest is rather shattered. On a buttress 150 feet northwest is a challenging route; climb the steep south face and overhang.
*Variation,* OFF TO SEE THE WIZARD, 5.9. Face and roof.

## Doorway Rocks

The Doorway Massif is perhaps the most expansive cliff area at Devil's Lake. When one sees it from the parking and picnic area at the south end of the lake its 200-foot height captures the eye and staggers the imagination. Despite its first appearance, the area is quite broken up. The tallest vertical walls are about 60 feet. The unique feature of the area is the possibility of multiple-pitch climbing, with mountain-type scrambling and route finding. A large gully divides the Massif into Major Mass and Minor Mass.

Major Mass includes the distinctive Devil's Doorway formation and is further divided into an Upper Band and a Lower Band. The two bands are separated by a terrace and ledge system that in places contains a 20 foot middle band of rocks.

Minor Mass consists mainly of a single large buttress with two distinct levels. The lower (south) level reaches a high point designated the South Tower. The saddle behind South Tower is accessible by a short climb from either side.

Red Rocks is east of Doorway Rocks along the Potholes Trail. This accessible area is often used by beginner groups, though its location right on a hiking trail is an unfavorable feature.

Ramsay's Pinnacle consists of the rock outcroppings immediately west of the main Doorway Massif.

APPROACH: Hike up the talus slope to the base of the Lower Band or hike part way up the Potholes Trail, then traverse 100 yards west to the base of the Minor Mass and the Keyhole. When approaching from above, use the short scenic trail that dips down from the Devil's Doorway Trail, giving access to Devil's Doorway and the top of the Upper Band. Descend the gully between Major Mass and Minor Mass, or a broken section west of Major Mass, to reach the lower level.

## MAJOR MASS, UPPER BAND (Diagrams 32 E and 33 E)

Devil's Doorway has several interesting climbs on its twin pillars. It is the scene of many dramatic demonstrations of rock-climbing techniques to passing tourists. The northwest corner, Romper (route 1), or Doorway Chimney (route 3), are usually used to ascend to set upper belays.

I     ROMPER, 5.2. Climb ledges at northwest corner of the formation.

**2**　LAZY DAY, 5.7. Climb north face near left edge.

**3**　DOORWAY CHIMNEY, 5.2. The chimney walls have been worn smooth by the boots and butts of many climbers. Those with long legs may feel unpleasantly cramped.

**4**　IMPOSSIBLE CRACK, 5.8. Start on wall below crack, climb overhang to crack, then jam or layback to top.
*Variation,* 5.7. Start inside the Doorway, climb left to crack (half the battle), then follow crack to top.

**5**　UP YOURS TOO, 5.8. Climb south end of the south pillar.

**6**　BLOODY FINGER, 5.6. Climb southwest side of the south pillar. A fall from this knife-edge crack can be messy.

**7**　5.6. Climb southwest side of the north pillar.

UPPER BAND. Several gullies can be used to descend from the trail to the base of the Upper Band; the most convenient is reached by route 16.

**8**　5.5. Crack.

**9**　5.2. Crack.

**10**　THE THREE KINGS, 5.7. Three large blocks form a ridge at the east end of the Upper Band. Climb the short strenuous layback between the west and middle King.

**11–15**　This small buttress has several short routes. The MAGICAL MYSTERY TOUR is for beginners. Start at low point near south corner (route 13) climb southeast side to base of huge detached block, traverse around south end of the buttress onto slanty ledge (route 14); climb up behind the detached block and scramble to top.

**16**　4th-class access route.

**17**　HIDDEN WALL, 5.8. The headwall between two prominent buttresses. Climb the face and overhang.

**18**　THE CRYPT, 5.2. Is it actually possible to escape from this rock tomb? Start in gully below, climb a narrow chimney past chockstone into the crypt.

**19**　5.4. From base of The Crypt (route 18), traverse left to an open alcove and stem to top.

**20**　FAITH, HOPE AND CHARITY, 5.4. Start from bottom of east face, follow crack past small overhang.

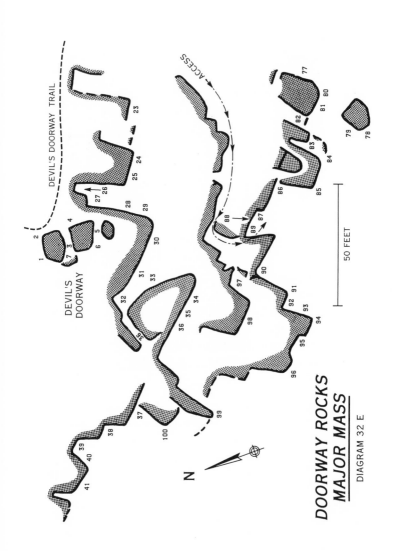

## DOORWAY ROCKS
## MAJOR MASS

DIAGRAM 32 E

DEVIL'S DOORWAY TRAIL

DEVIL'S
DOORWAY

ACCESS

50 FEET

N

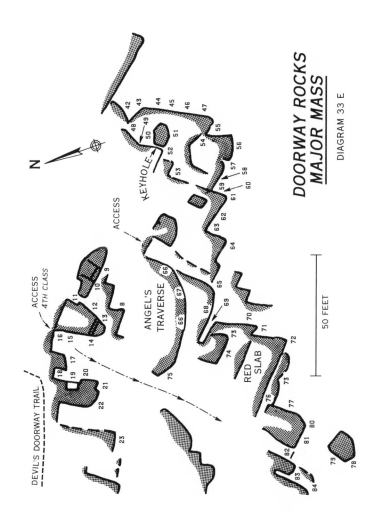

N

DEVIL'S DOORWAY TRAIL

ACCESS
4TH CLASS

ACCESS

KEYHOLE

ANGEL'S
TRAVERSE

RED
SLAB

*DOORWAY ROCKS*
*MAJOR MASS*

DIAGRAM 33 E

50 FEET

141

**21** ANGEL'S CRACK, 5.6. A dihedral marked by a steep arrowhead slab. Climb past the slab, exit right to top.

**22** THE JOLLY ROGER, 5.8. Climb the southwest face, following crack system past two small niches.

**23** 5.4. Crack and corner.

**24** MARY JANE, 5.8. Climb right side of south face to last ledge, then (crux) step onto toehold at right corner and reach for finger jam.

*Variation,* 5.6. Start as above, traverse left to good ledge at west corner, mantle to top.

**25** ROSEMARY'S BABY, 5.12b. Climb face 8 feet left of Mary Jane (route 24).

**26** 5.2. Chockstone chimney. Possible access route.

**27** VAMOS ALA KAMA, 5.5. Crack.

**28** INDECISION, 5.4. Climb cracked face, ending below blocks at south end of Devil's Doorway. Two distinct lines are possible, but most climbers zigzag, finding the easiest way.

**29** SPLIT DECISION, 5.7. Climb crack and face 3 to 4 feet left of Indecision (route 28) to large ledge. Finish in notch above ledge.

**30** CEDAR TREE WALL, 5.4. There are two crack climbs on this wall. Start behind cedar tree, climb right crack past pine tree to top. The left crack ends short of the top. Complete the route by climbing a short wall.

**31** CANNABIS SATIVA, 5.8. Climb face on small holds and finish in crack above.

JUNGLE GYM TOWER (routes 33–36) stands out slightly from the wall behind it. To reach the climbs from above, descend the gully (route 32) on the east side of the tower.

**32** 4th-class descent route.

**33** 5.4. Climb east face of Jungle Gym Tower from the gully.

**34** JUNGLE GYM, 5.4. Start on top of the Seventh Buttress (western buttress) of the Lower Band, climb up jam crack to a ledge, then up to a sloping platform. Mantle up on west side of the platform and climb to top of the tower.

**35** DANCES WITH FIBS, 5.7. Climb face left of bulge to overhang. Mantle overhang (crux), continue to top.

**36** JUNGLE GYM CHIMNEY, 5.4. Start climb below pine

tree. Climb 15 feet, then traverse left across a slab, using flake handholds, continue up chimney behind west side of Jungle Gym Tower.

**37**   THE PLAYGROUND, 5.5. Don't forget to look over there! A not-too-steep face for practice on small hold technique.

**38–41**   Short climbs.


## MAJOR MASS, LOWER BAND
### (Diagrams 32 E and 33 E)

The KEYHOLE (routes 42–59) is the easternmost buttress of the Lower Band. Most of the climbs cross one of two platforms on the north and south sides of the Keyhole.

**42**   SUNKEN SLAB, 5.6. Start at recessed section, well up along the base of the buttress. Climb the approximate center of lower slab to overhang, step up onto lip of overhang and then up slab to a stance. Traverse left to short jam crack beneath highest overhang and exit left.

**43**   PROSPERITY, 5.4. Begin in the crack just left of the Sunken Slab (route 42), angle left, following good holds up the outside corner.

**44**   HAMMER CRACK, 5.8. There was a tradition (best forgotten) of using a wedged piton hammer to aid this climb. Climb crack straight up from bottom to North Platform. *Variation,* 5.6. Traverse from right into the crack 5 feet up.

**45**   MEAT HAMMER, 5.12b. Start climbing with one good handhold. Continue on face with very thin holds a few feet left of Hammer Crack (route 44) straight to the top.

**46**   HAMMER CASE, 5.12a. Same start as Meat Hammer (route 45). From good hold climb up and left, following crack to top.

**47**   HAMMER MASTER, 5.11d. Climb small overhang, move left, and follow crack on left part of wall.

**48**   5.5. At north edge of platform climb up and right above Sunken Slab (route 42).

**49**   5.7. Start in a slabby groove, climb to overhanging crack that leads to an inside corner.

**50**     TOP SHELF, 5.7. Start on face just left of the Keyhole. Climb face to an undercling, then left and up to ledge under a roof. Traverse left, escaping the roof, onto a sloping shoulder, continue up southeast ridge above the Keyhole.

**51**     NONCONFORMIST, 5.7. Start on ledge level with base of the Keyhole, climb southeast face of Keyhole Pillar.

**52**     KEYHOLE CHIMNEY, 5.4. Scramble up ledges to base of the Keyhole. Move up the crack to reach hold and swing into the chimney. Alternatively, traverse around outside of the Keyhole Pillar and enter chimney from the north. Exit from chimney onto south face and climb to top of the buttress, or climb awkwardly high inside the Keyhole and exit northeast.

**53**     5.4. Inside corner leading onto slab at top of Keyhole Buttress.

**54**     5.4. Climb mostly broken rock above east end of the South Platform to ledge where Nonconformist (route 51) starts. It is interesting to traverse right onto the steep east face and climb past a small pine tree to reach the same ledge.

**55**     STETTNER'S OVERHANG, 5.6. Start below right side of ceiling. Use holds to right of the deep crack (staying in the crack is harder), climb past the ceiling, then follow the crack over a mild overhang to the South Platform.

**56**     5.2. An easy face route to the South Platform.

**57**     EASY STREET, 5.0. The easiest route to the South Platform. Climb the obvious block-filled chimney.

**58**     5.6. Thin crack.

**59**     HARD TIMES, 5.4. Inside corner with small overhang 20 feet up.

The following climbs, King's Corner (route 60) and Wicker Man (route 61), cross part way up.

**60**     KING'S CORNER, 5.6. The corner is not climbed directly from the bottom; instead, start from right inside corner of Hard Times (route 59) and traverse onto the corner 12 feet up. Up corner past overhang, step right to hanging crack in east face (can be avoided by staying left of corner), up crack, then regain corner and follow it to top of crowning pinnacle.

*Variation*, 5.8. From left side of first ledge of Dippy Diagonal (route 62), traverse onto corner 12 feet up. Continue climb as above.

**61**  WICKER MAN, 5.12b. Climb overhanging corner directly. At 20 feet, move right to east narrow face. Continue up face with thin cracks, avoiding the wide hanging crack noted in King's Corner (route 60). Finish on face of top pinnacle.

**62**  DIPPY DIAGONAL, 5.7. Climb the crack that diagonals slightly left.

*Variation*, 5.8. Start on first ledge (15 feet up), to the right of Dippy Diagonal. Climb face and thin crack, through a niche, ending on next large ledge.

**63**  KENOSIS, 5.4. Climb crack and inside corner to second large ledge (pine tree), then up between awkward blocks above the inside corner.

**64**  5.3. Climb broken buttress left of Kenosis (route 63).

**65**  5.1. Access couloir.

**66**  ANGEL'S TRAVERSE, 5.4. An exposed ledge spanning the upper mass of a high rounded buttress, ordinarily used for walking on. Start traversing from head of access couloir (route 65). At the far (west) end of the traverse climb a chimney 20 feet to top of the buttress.

**67**  5.7. Climb buttress, starting in middle of traverse.

**68**  5.8. Start on ledge 30 feet below Angel's Traverse (route 66) The ledge is reached easily from left chimney, route 69. Climb crack up to west end of Angel's Traverse.

*Variation*, 5.7. Start at same point, climb diagonally right until a holdless section forces you farther right toward the access couloir (route 65).

**69**  5.2. Chimney.

**70**  INNOCENCE, 5.7. The steep east face of Red Slab Buttress. Start near dihedral (route 71), climb 15 feet, move right, then up center of face to slabbier rock above.

**71**  5.4. Climb dihedral or adjacent crack to top of the red slab.

**72**  5.4. Start at lowest point below southeast corner of the buttress, climb left onto a pedestal, step right back to the corner and up the red slab.

**73** RED SLAB, 5.4. Climb the slightly overhanging system of good holds, continue up the red slab. Move around corner to the right and climb southeast corner.

**74** 5.4. Same start as Red Slab (route 73), finish on southwest side, doing a mantle and balance step to reach top. Continue on short wall above.

**75** 5.9. A short face (boulder problem).

**76** CHOCKSTONE CHIMNEY, 5.4. You can raise the standard of this route by starting in the inside corner; otherwise simply walk up from the right on ledges. Stem past the large chockstone into the chimney above.

**77** TM OVERHANG, 5.9+. Climb the tough layback crack on the east face to a resting place just below the overhang. Reach for good holds above the overhang, then merely pull yourself up until footholds are found.
*Variation*, 5.8. Exit left of overhang.
*Variation*, 5.10b. At overhang, move right, then continue straight up to top.

**78** LAYBACK BOULDER, 5.6. This is a large boulder that impedes travel along the base of the Lower Band. Start on southwest side, swing right onto south slab, then layback to top. Descend on the northeast side of the boulder.

**79** 5.4. Short jam crack.

**80** 5.6. Start on slabby rock at southeast corner of the buttress, climb onto a shelf above first overhang, traverse left onto southwest face. Continue as in Archway Cookie (route 81).

**81** ARCHWAY COOKIE, 5.8. Start on southwest face above the large boulder. Climb past bulge, using friction handholds, move up under the arching overhang, traverse right around the arch, then climb to top of the buttress.

**82** 5.2. Descent route from Archway Buttress.

**83** 5.4. Chimney route.

**84** BLUE SLAB, 5.4. Start at southeast corner (pine tree on first ledge), ascend the giant staircase to the blue slab at the top.

**85** 5.4. Start at west corner, climb up and right more or less as above.
*Variation*, 5.5. Climb left into a wide-angling crack on the west face.

**86** 5.4. Chimney route.

**87**   5.4. Inside corner crack.

**88**   MENTAL BLOCK, 5.12a/12b. Overhanging red wall. Start on left part of wall, climb up and right. At center of wall, climb directly to top.

**89**   Access gully to top of the Lower Band. Start from the little inside corner, climb into the dirt gully, then up and right to top of the band.

**90**   CAT WALK, 5.7. Start in the inside corner, climb up and traverse left on an irregular ledge, then up near left corner.

**91–96**   SEVENTH BUTTRESS of the Lower Band. The last or westernmost buttress, it is the start of an easy four-pitch route that includes Jungle Gym Tower. The lower section is broken with many variations.

**97**   5.7. Inside corner (an unpleasant layback) or adjacent crack that leads into the inside corner.

**98**   NO REST FOR THE WICKED, 5.8. Start just left of pine tree, climb southwest face past three triangular pockets.

**99**   RIGHT ON, 5.4. A narrow, tall buttress or ridge. Start at inconspicuous point behind oak tree, climb past overhang, finish on either corner of the more prominent upper section.

**100**   5.7. Corner 10 feet left of upper section of Right On (route 99).

## MINOR MASS (Diagram 34 E)

**1–4**   East Buttress of Minor Mass. This small formation is separated from the main buttress by a grungy gully and has a few easy climbs for beginners.

**5**   OBDURACY, 5.6. Start right of oak tree, climb short wall to ledge above.

**6**   DISINCLINATION, 5.4. Start on first ledge left of the grungy gully, climb to large pine tree and up the inclined chute behind the tree.

*Variation,* 5.6. Climb overhanging blocks to right of the tree.

**7**   POWER OF A GOOD HAIRCUT, 5.12b. Start on same ledge as Disinclination (route 6), 10 feet right of Lady-fingers (route 8), climb straight to top.

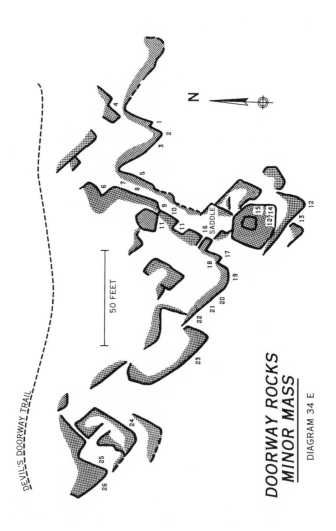

DEVIL'S DOORWAY TRAIL

N

50 FEET

## DOORWAY ROCKS
## MINOR MASS

DIAGRAM 34 E

**8** LADYFINGERS, 5.10a. Start on same ledge as Disinclination (route 6). Climb the wall into a shallow groove, then follow groove to top.

**9** PIGEON ROOF, 5.6. Climb crack leading to a prominent roof, pass the roof easily to wide crack above. The crack is that perplexing "in-between" width—too small to chimney and too large to jam.
*Variation,* 5.8. Traverse left under the roof, continue to top.

**10** NO STRANGER TO THE FIST, 5.12d. Climb face and overhang left of Pigeon Roof (route 9).

**11** FLOTSAM AND JETSAM, 5.4. This is actually two climbs, both starting in the recess. The left chimney is obstructed by a partially toppled tree. The right inside corner is longer, and has a good continuation on a small tower.

**12** B-MINOR MASS, 5.4. A delightful two-pitch climb to the top of South Tower. Begin on the south corner (lowest point of Minor Mass), climb to first good ledge, traverse left to small overhang. Continue here to next ledge, traverse right and climb the inside corner.

**13** 5.6. Climb face on southwest side to first ledge.

**14** 5.7. Start on ledge, climb southeast corner.

**15** IN THE HEAT OF THE SUN, 5.10a. Start on the first ledge, climb center of east face.

**16** 5.4. The chockstone chimney is the obvious route from the saddle, giving access to (or from) the scree ledges above.

**17** 5.3. From saddle, traverse left along a narrow ledge into second inside corner, then up a set of ledges.

**18** Á CHEVAL, 5.6. Start in the gully below the saddle and climb the sharp corner, avoiding the left inside corner on the left. Near the top you may find it helpful to mount up and ride.

**19** 5.7. Start on rounded corner, climb slabby wall past right end of upper overhang.

**20** GREEN LEDGES, 5.7. Climb the wall with three ledges 8 to 10 feet apart. From the highest ledge go around right corner, climb to overhang and into groove above.

**21** MR WIZARD AND TUTOR TURTLE, 5.10d. Start up face right of Manhandler (route 22), at overhang climb up and left to top.

**22** MANHANDLER, 5.9. Start 5 feet right of inside corner below a formidable overhang, climb up and right under overhang. Climb overhang and continue in crack above.

**23–26** Short climbs.

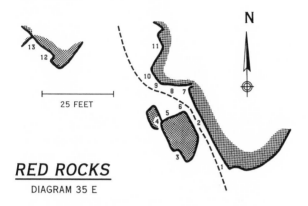

## RED ROCKS

DIAGRAM 35 E

## RED ROCKS (Diagram 35 E)

This small area is along the Potholes Trail, where it passes between a tower and a wall. The tower is usually ascended by stemming in the cleft above the trail (route 2, 5.4) or by the southwest dihedral (route 3, 5.4). Once on top there is an easy descent (route 4, 5.2), but it is more fun to lean across and step over the trail to the opposite wall. There are other good beginner climbs on these rocks; e.g., route 7, 5.3 (chimney) and route 9, 5.4 (ledge/jam crack). For a more challenging climb try the overhanging section left of the chimney (route 8, 5.9), or a corner farther left (route 10, 5.8).

## RAMSAY'S PINNACLE (Diagram 36 E)

The outcroppings west of Devil's Doorway consist of many low walls and towers. Ramsay's Pinnacle is 150 feet west of Devil's Doorway, with easy access from the Devil's Doorway Trail. There are a great number of short climbs; some are only marked on the diagram. You may find it interesting to explore, following the various terraces and gullies that give the area a rock garden character.

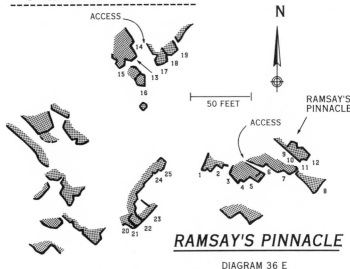

**RAMSAY'S PINNACLE**

DIAGRAM 36 E

**I**  5.7. Climb overhang and crack.

**2**  5.4. Inside corner.
*Variation,* 5.8. At 8 feet, move left and climb left side of face and upper corner.

**3–5**  5.3–5.4. Crack and corners.

**6**  5.5. Climb inside corner and narrow upper face.
*Variation,* 5.9. Start near left corner; avoid using right inside corner crack.

**7**  BLOODY SHIN, 5.7. Hanging inside corner. Climb up beneath roof 15 feet up. Move right and up to ledge. Continue in upper inside corner to platform below Ramsay's Pinnacle.

**8**  SUPER VGA, 5.9. Overhanging face. Start at low point at left end of wall, climb diagonally up and right to vertical crack. Follow crack to top.

**9**  5.4. Crack.

**10**  MONOCHROME, 5.8. Climb face, over both lower and upper overhang, finish left of chockstone.

**II**  RAMSAY'S RAMP, 5.7. Climb a series of overhanging, sloping steps, finish at chockstone.

**12**  5.7. Narrow face.

**13–16**  5.3–5.7. Don't overlook the climbs in or around the access gully.

**17**  5.7. A nice smooth face; avoid using crack or corner.

**18–19**  5.3–5.7. Don't overlook the climbs in or around the access gully.

**20–25**  5.3–5.9. Routes west of the gully, providing a great variety of short climbs. Routes 21–23 offer the biggest challenge.

## Balanced Rock Area

The Balanced Rock Area is more or less directly above the parking and picnic area at the south end of Devil's Lake. It is located at the corner or ridge (facing southwest) formed by the right-angle bend in the bluff. Access is by Balanced Rock Trail, which starts just across the railroad tracks north of the south shore parking and picnic area.

The main climbing interest is centered halfway up the bluff on Balanced Rock Wall. There are a large number of routes, a few up to 60 feet in length. A drawback to climbing here is the generally heavy trail traffic along the base of the wall. Box Canyon, an alcove behind the east end of Balanced Rock Wall, has some entertaining little climbs. There are other scattered climbing rocks on the upper half of the bluff, mostly to the east of Balanced Rock Wall.

## BALANCED ROCK WALL (Diagram 37 E)

**1**  BASSWOOD CHIMNEY, 5.2. A bit awkward until a ledge 20 feet up, thereafter quite easy.
*Variation*, 5.5. Climb to ledge as above, then climb crack 5 feet right of chimney.

**2**  MORNING AFTER, 5.10d. Start at left edge of the basswood thicket, climb face to reach a bucket hold 20 feet up.

**3**  NIGHT BEFORE, 5.11d. Climb face between Morning After (route 2) and Watermarks (route 4) on thin holds.

**4**  WATERMARKS, 5.8. The classic climb of the area. It appears on the "must" list of every aspiring climber. Start where the trail from below joins Balanced Rock Wall.

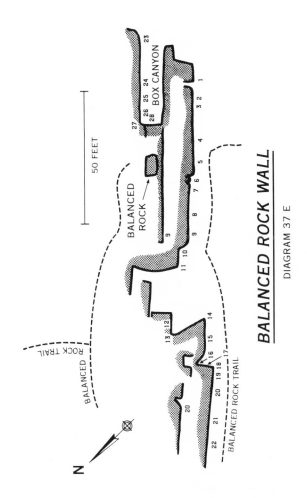

## BALANCED ROCK WALL

DIAGRAM 37 E

50 FEET

N

BALANCED ROCK TRAIL

BOX CANYON

BALANCED ROCK

BALANCED ROCK TRAIL

153

Climb up 10 feet to a ledge, right to crack with two triangular pocket holds, up crack past bulge (crux), and continue to top.

WATERMARKS DIRECT, 5.10a/10b. Start directly below the triangular pockets, climb straight up.

WATERMARKS LEFT SIDE, 5.8. Start as in Watermarks, at ledge, climb up and slightly left into a small inside corner below an overhang, step out right, and the rest is easy.

**5** DER GLOTZ, 5.9. Start on the face 10 feet left of Watermarks (route 4) below a faint slanting dihedral a few inches wide. Follow this line past the left end of the overhang noted in Watermarks Left Side (route 4 variation).

DER GLOTZ DIRECT, 5.9. Same start as Der Glotz. Climb straight up, staying close to left corner of wall and avoiding left corner.

**6** SUNKEN PILLAR, 5.5. Start at the double cracks, stem up until the cracks diverge, follow either crack. The climb ends near the base of Balanced Rock.

**7** AAHRG, 5.9+. Start at the large oak, climb face straight up to the pulpit.

**8** RED PULPIT, 5.6. Start at a thin crack 5 feet left of the two oak trees. Climb crack (harder for shorter people), then step right onto the pulpit 20 feet up, continue left and up past a juniper to top.

**9** FEAR AND TREMBLING, 5.9. Start on face just right of corner. The first 10 feet is quite difficult. Continue up crack and wall (close to corner) to large ledge 15 feet below top. Finish on or near corner of upper 15-foot wall. *Variation,* 5.10d. Climb center of upper 15-foot wall through flaring crack.

**10** NEW BOX, 5.4. Climb the inside corner until it becomes a crack, continue up crack or step right to easier rock.

**11** MR NEUTRON, 5.6. Climb the wall and corner, stay left of inside corner.

**12** 5.9. Start from dirt and rock slope on the left side of the gully. Climb the wall, a couple of feet right of inside corner, into a shallow dihedral (crux), then to top.

**13** 5.4. Inside corner with projecting chockstone.

**14** GRANDMA'S STAIRCASE, 5.6. Climb the corner on

easy ledges to overhang (leave grandma here). Step right and climb face left of route 13 inside corner to top.

**15**    SPRING FEVER, 5.8. This is not a clearly defined line. Start up center of steep lower slab to the overhang. Do not go into the niche of Bifurcation (route 16); instead, step up right past the overhang. Continue by laybacking the steep narrow section above (note the loose flake hold).

**16**    BIFURCATION, 5.2. Climb the slab through notch on left side (chockstone in notch) into alcove above. Step left onto a boulder bench and continue to top.
*Variation,* 5.6. Climb right crack inside the alcove.

**17**    MOONDUST, 5.11b. Climb overhanging wall with crack; avoid using the right wall.

**18**    JOY RIDE, 5.9. Overhanging corner.

**19**    RIDERS ON THE STORM, 5.10c. Face between Joy Ride (route 18) and Invitation (route 20).

**20**    INVITATION, 5.6. Start below the obvious crack, climb crack to bench above. Walk off or climb onto a sharp block and retable to top.
INVITATION DIRECT, 5.8. Start same as Invitation; follow thin crack left into notch at top of the wall.

**21**    R.S.V.P., 5.9. Climb straight up wall into the notch noted in Invitation Direct (route 20).

**22**    5.8. Climb short wall 5 feet from west end.


## BOX CANYON (Diagram 37 E)

**23**    5.4. A relatively long route that starts at low point of the wall below Box Canyon. Climb the corner and somewhat slabby wall 35 feet to a ledge, up an easy inside corner to another ledge, then any of several continuations to top.
*Variation,* 5.6. At the 35-foot ledge, step left and climb the obvious jam crack.

**24**    WHAMUS, 5.4. Climb right crack in the north wall of Box Canyon.

**25**    HITCH HIKE, 5.4. Climb left crack.

**26**    BALANCE CLIMB, 5.7. Climb the smooth wall (about 5 feet right of the inside corner) to the level of Balanced Rock platform. Continue the same line over a bulge to platform above.

**27**   THE GARGOYLE, 5.4. Climb the inside corner past the projecting chockstone, or traverse left to Balanced Rock. *Variation,* 5.4. Starting from Balanced Rock, do a "blind" traverse into the inside corner, then up past the chockstone, as above.

**28**   5.6. Short jam crack that leads to Balanced Rock.

## BALANCED ROCK RIDGE (No Diagram)

A series of walking and scrambling pitches, leading from Balanced Rock to the bluff top 200 feet above. Balanced Rock itself can be ascended on the east side or northeast corner. It is a one-move climb, especially if you are tall enough to reach the top.

## ROCKS EAST OF BALANCED ROCK WALL (No Diagram)

There are rocks east of the immediate Balanced Rock area. The East Bluff elevation drawing, West End, will help you locate the rocks.

Walk around the east end of Balanced Rock Wall and up the gully 100 feet; on the right is a 45-foot high outcropping with an overhanging summit block and a south-facing lower wall.

LIEDERKRANZ, 5.9. Climb right crack and ledges on south wall. At horizontal crack, just above the lower overhanging block, traverse left to west corner. Follow corner to top.

BEAR HUG, 5.11c. Same start, but climb the south face of the lower overhanging block to horizontal crack. Finish on west corner.

KRANZ, 5.6. Climb left layback crack leading up the west side of outcropping.

*Variation,* 5.9. Halfway up, climb overhang on west side of lower block, finish on west corner.

THE SLAB, 5.4. Hike up lower bluff midway between Balanced Rock and Devil's Doorway. Above the main boulderfield is a 35-foot slab with two 5.4 routes.

THE EFFIE, 5.7. The name is a memorial to Effinger Beer, once brewed in Baraboo. It is above The Slab on a wall facing southwest. Climb inside corner/jam crack that starts with an overhang, negotiate the overhang without using the large detached block on the left.

5.7. Climb the face directly above the block on The Effie.

WHERE IS THE BEER, 5.10d. Climb overhang and face right of The Effie. Avoid using the good holds on the right.

The face left of The Effie has two routes.

5.10a. Left side of face.

5.11a. Right side of face.

## HOLE-IN-THE-WALL (Diagram 38 E)

This small area is located 300 feet east of Balanced Rock. The wall is facing southeast and has a few interesting climbs.

**1**    5.2. Chimney.

**2**    5.3. Climb left edge of flake, continue in wide crack on upper wall.

**3**    DON'T LEAN ON THE TREE, 5.8. Overhanging wall with thin crack on outside of flake.

**4**    5.7. Crack.

**5**    5.3. Climb leaning block, use chockstone behind right edge.

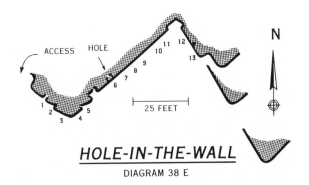

*HOLE-IN-THE-WALL*

DIAGRAM 38 E

**6**     HOLE-IN-THE-WALL, 5.6. Climb crack to niche, reach high, for jam hold, in left crack above niche. An attractive climb on smooth clean rock. The wall is slightly overhanging.

**7**     SURPRISE, 5.8. Climb a series of cracks diagonally up. Start 4 feet right of Hole-In-The-Wall (route 6). When level with niche, move right a couple of feet, continue to top. Do not use the edge of Hole-In-The-Wall niche.

**8**     LEFT ARM, 5.10a. Thin crack and flake system. Take great care using the flakes; they might peel off.

**9**     RODIN'S INSPIRATION, 5.7. Climb crack. The upper shallow inside corner is surprisingly harder than it looks.

**10**    THE WHITE CLOUD, 5.8. Face route starting 5 feet left of route 11.

**11**    5.4. Crack leading to shallow chimney.

**12**    5.4. Several cracks in short face.

**13**    5.5. Corner and face. Climb on or just left of corner.


# Railroad Tracks Area

Above the east shore of the lake, roughly midway between the south and north shores, are a number of outcroppings affording excellent climbing. Many of the climbs are down low, a feature that is appreciated on hot summer days. The major outcroppings are Railroad Amphitheater, Birthday Rocks, and Horse Rampart. These are all near the "electric fence," a net that parallels the railroad tracks for several hundred feet to give warning in the event of rock fall onto the track.

The Railroad Amphitheater is at the bottom of the bluff, 150 feet north of the electric fence. It is notable for its overhanging north wall and two fairly long climbs on its south wall. At an upper level is Waterfall Wall, a formation with rounded ledges and contours.

The Birthday Rocks are in the area above the electric fence. The main southwest wall starts 50 feet above the fence and angles up (southeast) to a prominent tower.

Horse Rampart is above the large boulderfield just south of the electric fence. It is a higher southward continuation of the band that forms the upper part of the Railroad Amphitheater and Birthday Rocks. The culminating point at the south end of the rampart is Teetering Tower. Other rocks in the area include Lothar's Ledges, a series of rock steps on the boulderfield above and south of the electric fence, and Squirrel's Nest Tower, a 50-foot formation 100 yards south of Horse Rampart.

## RAILROAD AMPHITHEATER (Diagram 39 E)

**1**  SNEDEGAR'S NOSE, 5.7. Ridge route. Start on right side of corner, step left and up onto block at base of the ridge, stem 10 feet on right side, continue steep slab climbing on, or just left of, ridge corner.

**2**  JACK THE RIPPER, 5.10c. For those who enjoy self-abuse. Start below a diagonal gash, jam up the gash, and reach ridge about halfway up the wall.

**3**  COP RIPPER, 5.12b. A difficult climb between Jack the Ripper (route 2) and Cop-Out (route 4).

**4**  COP-OUT, 5.11a. A study in combinatorial climbing. Start 10 feet left of The Pillar (route 6), climb thin cracks 35 feet into inside corner beneath overhang, step onto right corner, and climb to top.

**5**  CATENARY CRACK, 5.9. A swooping curve that yields to deep analysis. Start 5 feet left of The Pillar (route 6), climb crack to top of wall.

**6**  THE PILLAR, 5.6. Climb or chimney up the standing block, then step across into upper half of Catenary Crack (route 5).
*Variation*, 5.8. From The Pillar climb upper wall to the right of Catenary Crack.

**7–8**  Climbs on 20-foot wall above the northeast side of Railroad Amphitheater.

**9**  PINE TREE STEP-ACROSS, 5.6. Start 5 feet left of inside corner (Pine Tree Dihedral, route 10), climb onto first sloping ledge, shuffle left to corner, continue up and right onto overhanging block with pine tree, step *far* left and feel for handhold to pull yourself across, continue up slabby rock to top.
*Variation*, 5.6. Start in inside corner, but traverse left on black rock, then climb up to overhanging block with pine tree.

**10**  PINE TREE DIHEDRAL, 5.5. Climb the inside corner

below pine tree block, move right under the overhang and up to next ledge, continue in inside corner past two more ledges to top.

**11** 5.4. Inside corner.

**12** 5.7. Inside corners obscured by trees.

**13** OLD SHOES, 5.10c. Climb corner to overhang, pass overhang on right and continue up corner to top.

**14** FACE-OFF, 5.9. Start on upper right end of detached block, step left onto the face, move up and left toward corner where climbing becomes easier.

LUMBY RIDGE (route 15–18). The ridge is named after Harry Lumby, a former CMC president who suffered a heart attack on these rocks on a hot Saturday morning while exerting himself on a layback. The ridge consists of short pitches. The start is only a few feet from the RR tracks.

**15** 5.4. Climb onto loose upright plate and up crack to first platform. Continue as follows.

**16** 5.5. Climb chimney from bottom or traverse into it from adjacent inside corner, to reach next platform. Step across gap to the north, going around and into a short chimney, then up. Walk to next low wall.

**17** 5.4. Climb up onto a sloping platform.

**18** 5.4. Step onto left end of large displaced block, go right and up onto a little slab and climb to summit platform. A hole in the platform gives access to scramble route down south side.

**19** 5.4. Short corner.

**20** 5.5. Climb short face or right inside corner.

**21** 52. Corner next to wide chimney.

**22** THE TURRET, 5.7. Start on south corner below first overhang or on right side, climb or traverse onto corner above first overhang to reach ledge 15 feet up that extends to the left. Continue somewhat right on south side to top of the turret.

**23** 5.3–5.7. Short wall with two crack routes and one inside corner.

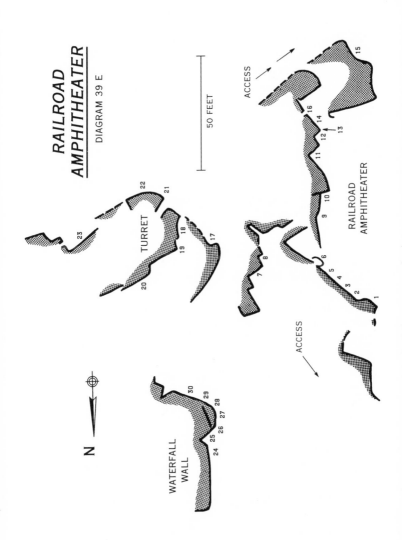

## RAILROAD AMPHITHEATER

DIAGRAM 39 E

50 FEET

N

RAILROAD AMPHITHEATER

TURRET

WATERFALL WALL

ACCESS

ACCESS

## WATERFALL WALL (Diagram 39 E)

**24**    5.7. Start up right diagonal ledge, climb crack to ledge beneath notched overhang, retable through the notch and up short steep wall to top.

**25**    5.6. Inside corner and chimney.

**26**    DISAPPEARING LEDGE, 5.7. Climb corner to large ledge, move right and step up on wall above, traverse left on a disappearing ledge, continue up and left around the corner.

**27**    5.9+/10a. Start 8 feet right of corner. Climb straight to top over upper overhang.

**28**    CHARLOTTE'S WEB, 5.10a. Start between blocks, climb V-niche straight up. Avoid use of large ledge (route 29).

**29**    5.8. Start on block and climb left to a large ledge, continue right and up, staying close to southwest corner.

**30**    SLIMER, 5.12a. Climb middle of overhanging wall.


## BIRTHDAY ROCKS (Diagram 40 E)

**I**    HORNER'S CORNER, 5.4. Climb crack 20 feet to a bench, then up west wall and southwest corner, climbing from ledge to ledge. Beware, sitting on a ledge is indecorous and subject to penalty.

**2**    5.7. Thin crack in recessed section.

**3**    PEEL OFF, 5.7. Climb crack system with shallow niche.

**4**    BOWING TO THE UNDERCLING, 5.12a. Climb short face with horizontal crack.

**5**    5.4. Ledges and crack that end left of 15-foot upper corner.

**6–7**    THE TWINS, 5.7. Both climbs are in shallow inside corners leading to an overhang.

**8**    GREAT WHITE HOPE, 5.11a. A difficult face to the left of Birthday Crack (route 9).

**9**    BIRTHDAY CRACK, 5.7. A prominent crack with overhang at ledge one-third of the way up.

**10**    BIRTHDAY CHIMNEY, 5.3. A long chimney leading all the way to top.

**II**    CAESARIAN WEST FACE, 5.12b/12c. Climb up cen-

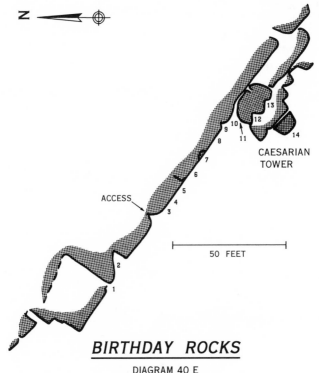

## *BIRTHDAY ROCKS*

DIAGRAM 40 E

ter of face, move left to pass small overhang. After a hard fingertip mantle to ledge, follow crack, then traverse left and up to flake. From flake, continue up and left to corner.

**12** CAESARIAN TOWER, 5.8. Start on first ledge, climb the sharp west corner or adjacent groove to higher ledge on northwest side, climb right onto the overhanging upper corner (the key is keeping hand in left crack), shinny to top of tower.

**13** SPECIAL DELIVERY, 5.6. Climb chockstone crack in the hanging inside corner.

**14** BIRTHDAY BOULDER, 5.9–5.10a. Face route with several variations.

Birthday Crack (diagram 40 E, route 9). Climber: Jan Marion. Photo: Alex Andrews.

# HORSE RAMPART (Diagram 4I E)

**I**   5.8. Corner above low slab.

**2**   BETWEEN THE SHEETS, 5.12c. Climb overhang, up and left past pin, continue on face to the top.

AAA, 5.12a. Climb "pumpy" overhang on corner to the top.

**3**   5.7. Climb the inside corner below first overhang, exit right onto south shoulder, then step left onto the exposed west face. Climb face, ending on northwest shoulder left of capstone.

**4**   MONARCH, 5.9. Climb steep slab (5.7), to vertical upper wall, then up small overhang into small dihedral. Traverse left to crack in sunken face.

**5**   THE HORSE, 5.4. Start by oak tree, climb up to left (east) end of large flake (The Horse), step right and mount The Horse (or vice versa), then up corner to top.

**6**   5.7. Start near corner and climb past west end of The Horse (route 5).

**7**   ARCHERY, 5.8. Climb face just left of pine tree up to The Horse (route 5).

**8**   ROGER'S ROOF, 5.8. Climb rib 4 feet right of pine tree to small ledge below crack in the roof, jam over the roof. Use a knee if it helps.

**9**   WOGERS WOOF WIGHTSIDE, 5.11c. Wander up to the roof. Climb overhang right of Roger's Roof (route 8); finish on face above.

**I0**   TREACHERY, 5.7. Waltz up 10 feet to ledge just right of alcove, step up left, painfully jamming left foot. Continue up narrow rib past birch tree, then into easy chimney.

*Variation,* 5.7. Climb lower wall, staying 6 feet right of the alcove.

**II**   LECHERY, 5.8. Climb crack to ledge at 25 feet, finish in thin crack on upper wall.

**I2**   DEBAUCHERY, 5.8. Pure climbing deficient in protection. Climb on or near corner for 25 feet past first ledge, move a few feet left, and pull onto a comfortable ledge. Above this point, the corner is ill defined. Continue slightly right into a shallow concavity for final 20 feet.

*Variation,* 5.8. Climb lower face right of corner to the comfortable ledge.

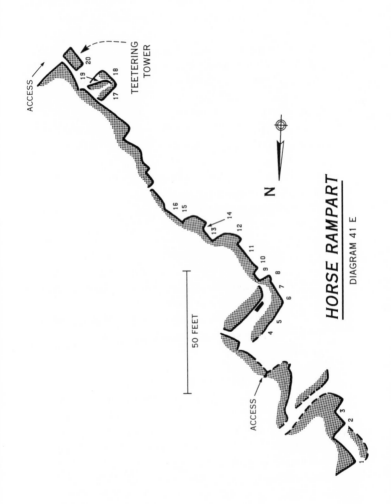

_HORSE RAMPART_

DIAGRAM 41 E

ACCESS

ACCESS

TEETERING
TOWER

50 FEET

N

1 2 3 4 5 6 7 8 9 10 11 12 13 14 15 16 17 18 19 20

*Variation,* 5.11d. Same start as first variation, but avoid the comfortable ledge and climb over the bulge and join Debauchery at the shallow concavity.

**13**   PRIMAK'S SURPRISE, 5.? To rate this climb would spoil the surprise. Every 10 feet you think you have passed the crux. Climb the inside corner, switch-backing holds on either side whenever helpful.

**14**   PLETHORA, 5.11a. Stem up the inside corner past slight bulge on left wall to ledge 20 feet from top, climb the ugly overhanging crack to a cedar tree.

PTOLEMY, 5.10d. Start just right of outside corner. Climb face until under roof, step up left around corner without using Plethora crack. Move up right and over roof. Exit on Plethora, Primak's Surprise (route 13), or route 15.

**15**   5.5. Up the inside corner onto left block, then up well-fractured rock to top.

**16**   VIA APIA, 5.7. Jam crack.

**17**   MUNG, 5.9. Crack system in northwest face.

**18**   5.8. Climb lower face to ledge, continue on left corner.

**19**   MOTHER SMUCKER'S JAM, 5.8. Overhanging jam crack.

**20**   TEETERING TOWER, 5.7–5.9. A 40-foot tower separated from the main wall by a jumpable gap. The climb on the northwest corner is 5.7, except for the start, which is 5.9. There was an easier start at the south corner until a hold broke off.

## LOTHAR'S LEDGES (No Diagram)

Named for Lothar Kolbig, a former CMC president who was active in the 1940s and 1950s. This is a series of three rock steps, on the boulderfield above and south of the electric fence and below Horse Rampart. There are a number of short climbs, including a fall across from the first tower to the next wall. It is good place for beginners, since each step has at least one easy climb.

## SQUIRREL'S NEST TOWER (No Diagram)

A 50-foot outcropping at midlevel on the bluff, 300 feet south of Teetering Tower (route 20) on Horse Rampart. It can also be approached from the opposite direction by contouring 600 feet north from Balanced Rock Wall. The southwest side has the following closely spaced routes (right to left):

5.7. Inside corner and hanging chimney near south corner.

5.7. Wide crack with remains of tree stump.

5.7–5.8. Left half of southwest face, two routes up the overhang.

5.9. Start from ledge on northwest side, step right to west corner, then up corner.

## North End of the East Bluff

There are several small rock outcroppings at the north end of the lake on the East Bluff, which offer a number of interesting but short climbs (20 to 25 feet). These areas are located close to the East Bluff Trail and are best approached from the north. They are Cabin Rocks, Elephant Rocks, Tomahawk Rocks, and Monolith Blocks.

APPROACH: The East Bluff Trail starts at the northeastern corner of Devil's Lake. From the North Shore Park entrance, drive east across the railroad tracks and turn south to the second or third parking lot. The trail starts across the road (east) between these two parking lots.

The two park-named rock formations along the East Bluff Trail are used to locate the climbing areas.

A. Elephant Rock is .35 mile from the start of the East Bluff Trail.

B. Tomahawk Rock is 550 feet farther south along the trail.

## CABIN ROCKS (No Diagram)

The four small, low outcroppings of Cabin Rocks are located above and just east of the parking lots at the northeast corner of Devil's Lake. The outcroppings start at parking lot level, 150 feet south of the yellow indoor toilet building, and rise gradually to the south. The southernmost outcropping is 250 feet north of Elephant Rock and 75 feet west of the trail.

On the southernmost outcropping there is an obvious, slightly overhanging, south-facing, inside corner (5.8) with a difficult, narrow face (5.11a) just to the left.

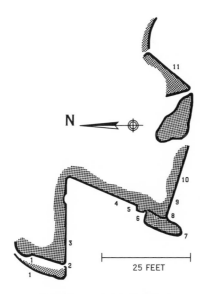

## ELEPHANT ROCKS

DIAGRAM 42 E

## ELEPHANT ROCKS (Diagram 42 E)

ACCESS: This small area is located west and across the trail from Elephant Rock.

| | |
|---|---|
| **1** | 5.5. Inside corner. |
| **2** | TRANSCENDENTAL DISFIGURATION, 5.10d. Sharp corner with crack. |

**3** CLEARASIL SPATTERED FANTASIES, 5.10b. Start in alcove and climb thin crack straight to top.
*Variation*, 5.8. Same start, but follow diagonal crack up and right.

**4** 5.8. Face route with down-sloping ledges, 5 to 6 feet left of crack.

**5** 5.7. Climb crack all the way to top.

**6** DUMBO, 5.9. Start up lower inside corner, continue on hanging pillar above to top. Avoid stepping on right platform.

**7** THE TRUNK, 5.7. Climb rib for 20 feet leading to inside corner, finish in corner.

**8** TOMB OF THE UNKNOWN HOMO, 5.7. Crack and chimney.

**9** TWO FINGER CRACKS, 5.10a. Climb, staying close to the two thin cracks. Don't wander off right.

**10** 5.7. Broken-up face and crack.

**11** ROMANCING THE BONE, 5.12b. Climb overhanging wall.

## TOMAHAWK ROCKS (Diagram 43 E)

ACCESS: The north end of Tomahawk Rocks is 250 feet south of Elephant Rock. This long, low outcropping stretches south 300 feet to Tomahawk Rock.

**1** 5.5. Climb crack.

**2** 5.4. Crack in inside corner.

**3** 5.8. Overhang with crack.

**4** 5.9. Short face route on lower part of wall.

**5** WINNEBAGO, 5.8. A nice face and crack route leading to top of wall.

**6** 5.10a. Climb slab and face to top.
*Variation*, 5.7. Climb lower face, move right to corner, follow corner to top.

**7** BRAVE, 5.9. Start in crack; when crack ends, move left and up.

**8** TEPEE, 5.9. Thin awkward crack.

**9** 5.8. Jam crack.

**10** 5.7. Thin crack starting as a layback.

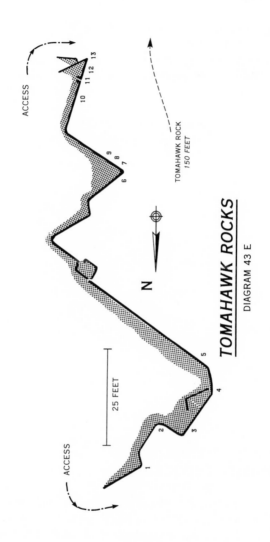

ACCESS

ACCESS

## *TOMAHAWK ROCKS*

DIAGRAM 43 E

N

25 FEET

TOMAHAWK ROCK
150 FEET

**11**    5.7. Crack too wide to jam and too narrow to chimney.

**12**    5.9. Climb narrow face just right of route 11 to top of wall.

**13**    MOHAWK, 5.8. Sharp corner.

## No Diagram

Two climbs are on a rock outcropping 75 feet south of Mohawk (route 13). Tomahawk Rock is located 80 feet farther south-southeast.

5.5. Inside corner facing south and west.

5.8. Face with hanging dihedral to the right.

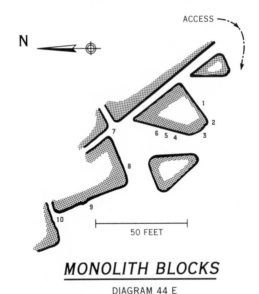

## MONOLITH BLOCKS

DIAGRAM 44 E

## MONOLITH BLOCKS (Diagram 44 E)

ACCESS: Monolith Blocks are 750 feet south of the Tomahawk Rock. Beyond Monolith Blocks are several low outcroppings of little interest to climbers.

**1**    5.7. Crack with a few nice layback moves.

**2**    THE QUILL, 5.9. Climb, staying on corner to top.

**3**    PORCUPINE, 5.9. Narrow face; avoid using the corners. *Variation,* 5.8. Same start, but make use of left corner.

**4**    5.9. Face just right of Foil (route 5), do not use crack.

**5**    FOIL, 5.8. Climb lower face to crack, continue in crack to top.

**6**    RAPIER, 5.11c. Start just right of corner or left of crack. Climb face without use of crack or left corner.

**7**    5.4. Wide crack/chimney.

**8**    5.6. Wide interesting crack.

**9**    SURFING WITH THE ALIEN, 5.11b. Climb the weakness in face. Start near left chimney, climb up and right.

**10**    5.4. Chimney.

## No Diagram

RUSTY CRACK, 5.7. 25 feet north of route 10. Climb rust-colored crack.

Small pink and purple buttress of weathered rock 150 feet south-southeast of Monolith Blocks.

RAINBOW CRACK, 5.9. Climb slightly overhanging jam crack hidden by trees.

Ten feet left (north) of Rainbow Crack are a couple of climbs.

5.5. Tight chimney.

5.8. Crack.

PINK PANTHER, 5.11b/11c. A few feet farther left (north) is a short wall with an overhang. Climb left of corner.

# The West Bluff

Climbing on the West Bluff has the same general character as climbing elsewhere at Devil's Lake. Like Quarry Rocks, the outcroppings are widely scattered and often obscured by trees, making it difficult to locate and identify particular outcroppings. For this reason a quite detailed description of the major rock groups and the approaches to them is presented below.

The West Bluff outcroppings show a banded structure which dips to the north in the same manner as the outcroppings on the opposite shore. For the most part, the bands are continuous; they consist of rock patches interrupted by wooden slopes. In a few places, the outcroppings form vertical extensions, providing relatively continuous ascent routes for 200 to 300 feet; e.g., Turk's Head Ridge and Prospect Point Towers.

## Major Rock Groups of the West Bluff

Stettner Rocks is located at the far south end of the West Bluff. It is a region with southeastern exposure, low elevation, and the advantage of a short approach. The rocks form a reddish band 200 feet long with climbs mostly short (20 to 30 feet), but of considerable variety. It is often used for instruction.

Lincoln's Chair is a minor rock cluster 300 feet north of Stettner Rocks, still on a relatively low section of the bluff. The climbs are 20 to 30 feet and on several levels, making it another suitable "school rocks."

Misery Rocks is above the cottages at the southwest corner of Devil's Lake. The traditional Fat Man's Misery climb is on the 40-foot summit wall of this region. The wall is distinguished by a large reclining block (The Pillow) that creates a cave-like enclosure. Directly below the summit wall is The Pantry, an outcropping with an alcove and ancillary walls and towers on two levels.

Dutchman Rampart is 100 feet north of Misery Rocks, across

West Bluff. Photo: Chuck Koch.

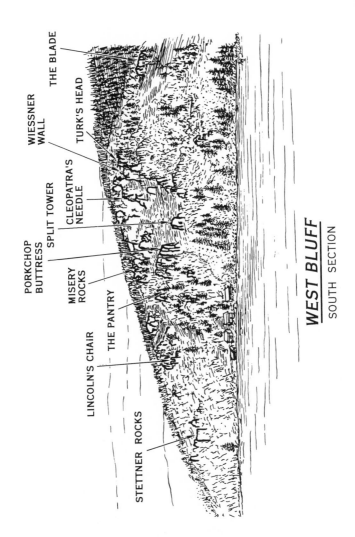

STETTNER ROCKS

LINCOLN'S CHAIR

THE PANTRY

MISERY ROCKS

PORKCHOP
BUTTRESS

SPLIT TOWER

CLEOPATRA'S
NEEDLE

WIESSNER
WALL

TURK'S HEAD

THE BLADE

## *WEST BLUFF*
SOUTH SECTION

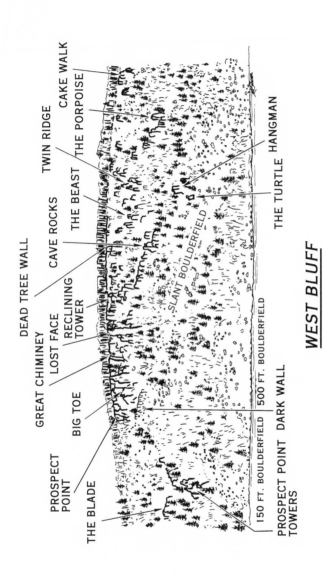

PROSPECT
POINT

THE BLADE

BIG TOE

GREAT CHIMINEY

LOST FACE

RECLINING
TOWER

DEAD TREE WALL

CAVE ROCKS

THE BEAST

TWIN RIDGE

CAKE WALK

THE PORPOISE

PROSPECT POINT DARK WALL
TOWERS

150 FT. BOULDERFIELD   500 FT. BOULDERFIELD

SLANT BOULDERFIELD

THE TURTLE   HANGMAN

## *WEST BLUFF*
MIDDLE SECTION

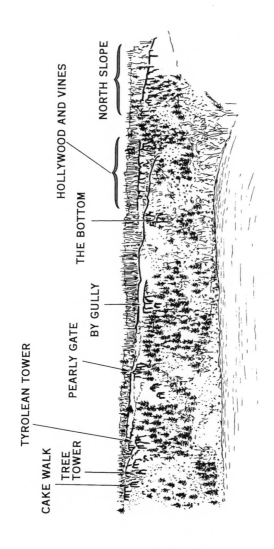

TYROLEAN TOWER

HOLLYWOOD AND VINES

NORTH SLOPE

THE BOTTOM

PEARLY GATE

BY GULLY

CAKE WALK

TREE TOWER

## *WEST BLUFF*
NORTH SECTION

Misery Gully. It features a prominent high roof, a south-facing wall, and a three-section tower, The Frigate. At a lower level are Dungeon Wall, Porkchop Buttress, and Split Tower. Porkchop Buttress is an impressive formation with relatively long climbs, 60 to 70 feet. Split Tower is an isolated 40-foot outcropping 150 feet north of Porkchop.

Cleo Amphitheater is part of the summit band on the south portion of the West Bluff. The Amphitheater is 200 feet across and partly surrounds a 50-foot spire, Cleopatra's Needle. These rocks are densely covered with routes.

Wiessner Wall and Turk's Head form a northerly extension of Cleo Amphitheater and are the most prominent of the southern rocks. Wiessner Wall is over 60 feet high, naturally broken into two pitches. Turk's Head can be seen in jutting profile from points along the south shore. The Blade is a separate outcropping 300 feet to the north.

Turk's Head Ridge ascends most of the bluff below Turk's Head, ending at Turk's Tooth. It provides a nearly continuous sequence of easy to moderate pitches.

Prospect Point Towers forms a ridge that extends up the middle third of the bluff below Prospect Point. It is a magnificent formation with fine climbs.

Prospect Point Rampart is the summit cliff on the central part of the West Bluff. The cliff is continuous for 400 feet from Prospect Point north to Lost Face. The average height of the cliff is 80 feet, but it is broken by many benches and ledges. In a few places it does provide long continuous climbs, notably at the Great Chimney and Lost Face. At the base near the south end is Dark Wall.

Reclining Tower and Dead Tree Wall are short separate sections of the summit cliff north of Prospect Point Rampart. The latter is the more impressive formation, consisting of a steep wall with climbs up to 60 feet.

From Reclining Tower, Cave Rocks Rampart extends northeast halfway down the bluff, ending at Cave Rocks. These rocks and those farther north (described below) are climbed quite infrequently.

Hangman Towers north of Dead Tree Wall consists of a group of towers, including Twin Ridge, The Porpoise, and other rocks scattered over several hundred feet on the upper half of the bluff. The climbs are all in the short category, up to 30 feet. The outcroppings end to the north, where a talus slope covers much of the upper bluff.

Tree Tower and Tyrolean Tower are 200 feet apart, both a little below the crest of the bluff. Behind Tree Tower there are summit walls of interest. The top of Tyrolean Tower was first reached by Tyrolean traverse.

North of Tyrolean Tower there are only a couple of isolated climbs until one reaches the region above the north end of the lake. Here the rocks consist of three distinct bands: By Gully, Hollywood and Vines, and North Slope. The most southerly, By Gully, has a few routes. The other two bands are more extensive, each extending several hundred feet immediately beneath the West Bluff Trail, with climbs typically 30 to 40 feet long.

# West Bluff Approaches

The present West Bluff Trail (summit trail) begins at the junction of the South Shore Road and the cottage access road, at the southwest corner of the lake; it is paved with asphalt. Formerly the trail began a few hundred feet to the east and is still usable. This old "climber's trail" is convenient for reaching some of the southern rocks of the West Bluff, since it follows the bluff crest more closely than the newer official trail. Useful landmarks along the West Bluff Trail (using the old variation to start) are described below. Distances noted below are between consecutive points.

## Old West Bluff Trail (Climber's Trail) and West Bluff Trail

A. The unmarked trail head is by the third utility pole along the cottage access road, 325 feet east of the South Shore Road.

B. 300 feet. The trail reaches a bench above the first minor rock band. Stettner Rocks is 100 feet northeast at this level.

C. 925 feet. The trail passes a vantage point that can be identified by a "slingshot" pine tree 50 feet east of the trail. The tree is growing on the summit wall of Misery Rocks. The trail passes a similar vantage point 300 feet before Misery Rocks, in the vicinity of Lincoln's Chair. Note: The Old West Bluff Trail joins the present West Bluff Trail. This is described under letter D.

D. 300 feet. The old trail merges with the new one above Cleopatra's Needle. A couple of short gullies, leading down to the Needle, are found by walking north along the rim. Wiessner Wall and Turk's Head are located 200 feet farther north. There is an unmarked path beaten down by hikers leaving the established trail above Turk's Head. This path gradually descends to the north for 400 feet until it passes above The Blade, then turns down and disappears in the gully adjacent to Prospect Point Towers.

E. 1000 feet. Prospect Point. This vantage point has a panorama that includes the whole of Devil's Lake. Prospect Point Rampart is the summit wall below and to the north of this point. To the south there is a broad summit boulderfield that occupies a hollow or break in the contour of the upper bluff.

F. 300 feet. Geodetic survey marker. A park service road goes west from here to join the South Shore Road. Great Chimney is 50 feet south of the marker. The access gully to Lost Face is 75 feet north. Reclining Tower is 175 feet north.

G. 425 feet. The trail passes Dead Tree Wall. There is an access gully south of the formation.

H. 425 feet. The trail passes above Go-Go Tower, 100 feet below. Twin Ridge is 150 feet south. These and the other rocks of Hangman Towers are not visible from the bluff top. About 200 feet to the north, on the upper bluff, is a boulderfield that reaches almost to the summit.

I. 425 feet. The trail passes Tree Tower. Though only 50 feet off the summit, the tower is easy to miss because of intervening trees; it has a small pine tree near its top.

J. 175 feet. An elevated vantage point, overlooking Tyrolean Tower, is barely discernible about 75 feet below. When approaching from the south there is a short rise in the trail.

K. 325 feet. Another vantage point. The rocks immediately below have no interesting climbs. However, 150 feet to the north, not visible from the trail, is Pearly Gate. Look for a narrow, descending cleft that leads 25 feet to the edge of the bluff above this wall.

L. 350 feet. The trail dips and crosses the head of a large gully. By Gully is about 100 feet down on the north side. Just north of the gully a path branches off from the summit trail and soon fades out.

M. 325 feet. Trail division point. The easterly branch is another false trail that follows a bench below the summit, eventually to become lost on a talus slope. It is often used, since one can continue down boulders directly to the north shore beach area. For a stretch this branch trail parallels the base of Hollywood and Vines, a summit band 200 feet north of the division point.

N. 650 feet. North Slope. A descending section of the trail about 225 feet long, with rock slabs along the edge of the bluff. The cliff below is the final rock band along the summit trail. The trail ends at the North Shore Road 375 feet farther north.

## Tumbled Rocks Trail (Shore Trail)

The Tumbled Rocks Trail starts at the south end of the West Bluff where the cottage access road ends. The most convenient and pleasant approaches using this trail are the following:

A. Cottage road. 200 feet before reaching the north end of the road, walk up (northwest) on the least overgrown talus in the area. This leads into a gully between Misery Rocks and Dutchman Rampart; walking straight up (west) leads to a gully south of The Pantry and Misery Rocks.

B. The trail head is at the end of the cottage access road. Double Chimney and Porkchop Buttress are 200 to 300 feet above this point. The easiest way to reach them is to go 100 feet north along the trail and follow a faint path up.

C. 350 feet. Turk's Head Ridge. Trail passes beneath the base of the ridge, a small tower 200 feet up the bluff.

D. The 150 Foot (wide) Boulderfield is the first open boulderfield that the trail crosses. Ascend the south edge of the boulderfield, turning a little south to reach the base of Prospect Point Tower, or hike the first 250 feet on a faint path in the woods just south of this boulderfield.

E. 500 Foot (wide) Boulderfield is 100 feet north of the 150 Foot Boulderfield. High above are the summit cliffs north of Prospect Point. Various sections of the cliffs can be reached as follows:

> 1. Ascend south edge of the 500 Foot Boulderfield, continue over and between large blocks onto the Slant Boulderfield (G) on the upper bluff. Follow the Slant Boulderfield southwest toward Prospect Point or go up through trees to the summit band in the vicinity of Great Chimney.

> 2. Ascend north edge onto the upper reach of the 500 Foot Boulderfield, then bear somewhat north to avoid most of the trees, passing a 25-foot rock with a steep slab climb. This brings you up to a low rock band, Cave Rocks Rampart.

Follow the rampart southwest to Reclining Tower, or cross it northwest to Dead Tree Wall.

F. The Turtle. North of the 500 Foot Boulderfield the trail passes through a gradually narrowing strip of trees. Near the north end of the strip, on the open slope (Slant Boulderfield) one can see The Turtle, a large sloping rock with a small boulder at the top. Cave Rocks is about 250 feet southwest of The Turtle. Hangman Towers covers an extensive area above The Turtle.

G. Slant Boulderfield. This is the third boulderfield that crosses the trail. It extends diagonally up and south, practically uninterrupted, following the tilt of the rock strata, to Prospect Point. Starting where the trail emerges from the trees, go up, across this boulderfield. Continue up on fairly open talus to The Porpoise, a rock band two-thirds of the way up the bluff. You can now veer north across a higher boulderfield to reach the summit in the vicinity of Tree Tower.

# West Bluff Rock Climbs

## STETTNER ROCKS (Diagram 1 W)

ACCESS: Starting from the cottage road, hike up the old West Bluff Trail 300 feet to a bench above the first minor rock band. On this level follow a path 100 feet northeast to base of Stettner Rocks.

**1**    5.8. Short face climb.

**2**    5.6. Overhang at southwest corner of west buttress. Climb left of a small sharp rib underneath the overhang.
*Variation,* 5.8. Climb right side of the rib.

**3**    5.2. Climb southwest corner on good ledges to top.

**4**    5.4. Climb 15 feet into easy upper chimney.

**5**    THE BROTHERS, 5.7. Southeast side of west buttress, a relatively unbroken face ascended on small ledges.

**6–9**    Short climbs.

**10**    THE NICHE, 5.4. Climb an inside corner to the niche, retable to the left or hand traverse farther left to an even easier spot.

There is a practice traverse between climbs 10 and 12 that is just off the ground and can be done unroped.

**11**    THE MANTLE SHELF, 5.8. Climb middle of wall to first ledge. The crux is climbing onto the smaller ledge 5 feet higher. An indirect approach is to traverse onto it from either end.

**12**    5.2. Chimney.

**13**    5.5. Follow bucket holds 2 feet right of the chimney, a bit overhanging.

**14**    5.9. Overhang on south side of Beastly Bulge (route 15).

**15**    BEASTLY BULGE, 5.7. An overhanging nose on the lower wall.

**16**    5.4. Wide crack.

**17**    5.5. Corner.

**18**    5.2. Buttress with easy ledges, continue on wall above.

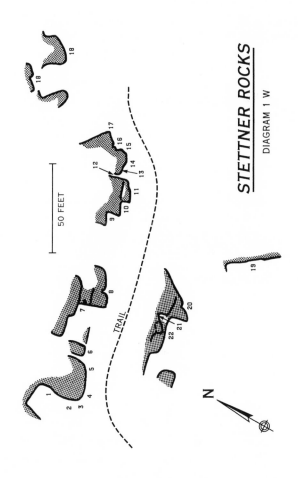

*STETTNER ROCKS*

DIAGRAM 1 W

50 FEET

N

TRAIL

## LOWER BAND (Diagram 1 W)

The following climbs are on some rather overgrown, dirty rocks below Stettner Rocks.

**19**   5.4. Crack in a wall facing southwest.

**20**   OLD PEW, 5.7. Start in diagonal crack, climb to first ledge, balance up carefully beneath overhang, reach into notch above and grope for a hold, surmount overhang.

**21**   5.4. Slabby chimney.

**22**   5.7. Detached block on upper wall. Follow midline of the block as closely as possible.

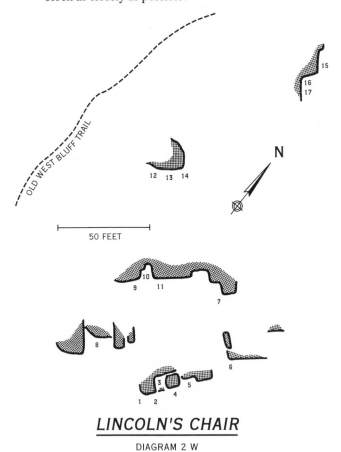

*LINCOLN'S CHAIR*

DIAGRAM 2 W

# LINCOLN'S CHAIR (Diagram 2 W)

ACCESS: Follow the old West Bluff Trail 625 feet beyond Stettner Rocks, descend 100 feet to Lincoln's Chair. It can also be reached from Misery Rocks; it is 200 feet south of The Pantry.

| | |
|---|---|
| **1** | LINCOLN'S CHAIR (south arm), 5.4. The two arms are 30 feet high and 10 feet apart. Start on south corner, end somewhat left around the corner. |
| **2** | 5.5. Southeast face of south arm. Start this slightly overhanging face from the right side where there is a hold that looks ready to break off. |
| **3** | 5.2. Short inside corner crack above seat of the chair. |
| **4** | LINCOLN'S CHAIR (north arm), 5.4. Start on left corner of the arm or (a bit harder) on little ramp on right corner. Climb about halfway up, then move right to pass overhang. |
| **5–7** | 5.2–5.4. Short climbs. |
| **8** | 5.2. Recessed slab. Climb face of slab or slant chimney on left side. |
| **9** | 5.4. Chockstone crack. |
| **10** | 5.3. Climb south wall of alcove. The north chimney of the alcove is a scramble. |
| **11** | 5.2. 35-foot wall. Best route is 10 feet north of the alcove. Farther north the wall is broken into short steps. |
| **12** | 5.7. Climb face 4 feet left of the wide crack (route 13). |
| **13** | 5.4. Climb wide crack. |
| **14** | TWO TOAD CORNER, 5.8. Climb just left of the corner to top. <br> *Variation,* 5.8. Start on right side of the corner, at 6 feet move back left. |
| **15** | 5.7. Minor wall 60 feet north of preceding outcropping. Climb 20-foot jam crack in a smooth face. |
| **16** | 5.4. Inside corner. |
| **17** | 5.7. Two cracks crossing a wide ledge. <br> *Variation,* 5.9. Climb lower left crack. |

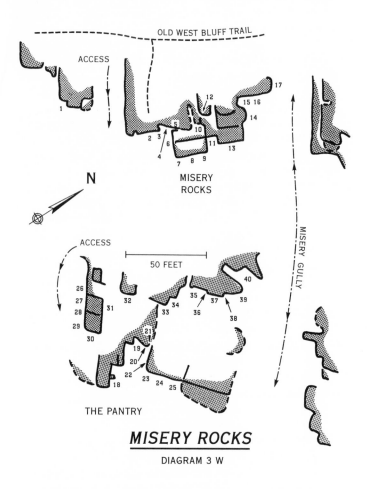

OLD WEST BLUFF TRAIL

ACCESS

1

12

17

15 16

14

5

10

2 3 6

11 13

4

7 8 9

N

MISERY ROCKS

ACCESS

MISERY GULLY

50 FEET

26
27
28
29
30

31

32

35
33 34 37 39
36

38

40

21

19

20

22 23 24 25
18

THE PANTRY

## MISERY ROCKS

DIAGRAM 3 W

## MISERY ROCKS (Diagram 3 W)

This wall forms the summit cliff in the region above the cottages. It is distinguished by a large reclining block, The Pillow, that forms a cave-like enclosure.

ACCESS: Walk up the old West Bluff trail .25 mile to the overlook above Misery Rocks. From the trail, the overlook can be identified by a "slingshot" pine tree.

From below, start up the bluff on the fairly open talus 200

feet before the end of the cottage road. This leads to the gully between Misery Rocks and Dutchman Rampart.

**1**   5.7. Start with layback move in a small inside corner, then climb easy rock above.

**2**   WEEPING WALL, 5.9. Start at a slight, ground-level niche, climb up, somewhat left, on small holds, then move back right, staying a few feet left of the adjacent crack (False Perspective, route 3).

**3**   FALSE PERSPECTIVE, 5.6. Shallow V-chimney and crack. Climb in chimney or on left outside corner. When chimney and corner join, follow crack to top.

**4**   WAILING WALL, 5.10c. Climb narrow wall between False Perspective (route 3) and Fat Man's Misery (route 5). Do not use the crack or holds of Fat Man's Misery. The lower part of the wall is slightly overhanging.

**5**   FAT MAN'S MISERY, 5.4. Start 10 feet inside "the cave" behind The Pillow. Climb the west wall until you get into a chimneying position facing east; work out of the cave and up to the tight chimney at the south end of The Pillow. The upper chimney becomes Any Man's Misery if you are trapped by leaning in too far.

**6**   PILLOWS EDGE, 5.8. South end of The Pillow. Start on pointed rock, climb the narrow south end of both lower and upper blocks; do not use holds on either corner.
*Variation,* 5.9. Start on ground right of pointed rock. Avoid use of pointed rock.

**7**   THE PILLOW, 5.6. Southeast corner and overhang. Climb corner to overhang formed by upper block. Climb overhang by moving a bit right and taking a high step.

**8**   5.3. Follow good holds left of center on The Pillow, escape right at overhang.

**9**   5.5. Climb at or near north edge of The Pillow.

**10**   SMOKE HOLE, 5.2. Climb deep chimney behind The Pillow, exit through hole at the top.

**11**   5.2. Chimney.

**12**   5.2. Narrow prominence above north end of The Pillow. Climb on south side or southeast ledges.

**13**   5.4. Three 10-foot steps taken at a crack that widens with each step.

**14**   5.7. Climb 10 feet to a ledge with a large tree, continue up right-hand corner. Go head-first into the tight awkward chimney or climb on outside just right of the chimney.

**15**   5.6. Long crack in left side of a dirty chute.

**16**   5.7. Overhanging wall. Start near north end, work left on ledges, then up to highest ledge.

**17**   5.8. Climb north end of the overhanging, lichen-covered wall.


## THE PANTRY (Diagram 3 W)

**18**   5.6. Corner/crack. Climb just left of corner to gain corner ledge, then angle right up the wide diagonal crack.

**19**   PANTRY SHELF, 5.8. Step up to the sloping shelf on the lower part of the wall, continue straight up and over the top overhang near the right corner.
*Variation*, 5.7. Same start, but follow shelf up and left into inside corner, continue up corner, passing final overhang on left.

**20**   PANTRY RIGHT, 5.9. Start 2 feet right of lower end of shelf in Pantry Shelf (route 19). Climb near right edge of wall to top.

**21**   5.1. Chimney with easy stemming.

**22**   5.3. North wall of The Pantry.

**23**   PANTRY CORNER, 5.4. A pleasant climb on well-spaced holds.

**24**   BREAD BOARD, 5.10b. Climb center of wall, starting in niche and finishing in flaky crack in highest part of wall.

**25**   5.4. Cracks.

**26**   5.2. Crack and inside corner.

**27**   K2, 5.9. Narrow face just left of Special K (route 28). Start with a very long reach, or more likely a jump, to reach the first hold. Continue on face above to base of small tower. Avoid using left corner.

**28**   SPECIAL K, 5.6. Climb a shallow chimney, overhang, and crack. End at a ledge near the top of a small tower.

**29**   5.8. Corner. Start behind pine tree, climb corner to top.

**30**   5.4. Climb southeast flank of the tower in three short pitches.

**31–34**   5.3–5.4. Short climbs.

**35**   5.7. Inside corner with small overhang.

**36** 5.2. Cracks.

**37** 5.5. Crack, narrowest at bottom.

**38** 5.6. Overhang. Climb around north end of overhang into inside corner.

**39** 5.7. Start on face or in angling crack just left of northeast corner. Climb 15 feet to a ledge, then up northeast corner on sloping holds.

**40** 5.4. Climb right wall of wide chimney.

Fifty feet below (southeast of) The Pantry there are several small buttresses with some interesting short climbs.

## DUTCHMAN RAMPART (Diagram 4 W)

ACCESS: Follow directions to Misery Rocks. Dutchman Rampart is immediately north of Misery Rocks.

**1** 5.6. Overhanging crack.

**2** 5.4. Deep covered chimney. Getting out at the top is a messy procedure.

**3** 5.6. Ledges/crack. Start on south side, left of the corner. Climb to second large ledge, finish by a finger crack in groove to left of Oh Rats roof (route 4).

**4** OH RATS, 5.8. Traverse north from the large ledge noted in route 3 and climb a layback underneath the large, upper overhang. Escape by traversing to the right-hand (north) corner. End with delicate climbing just around the corner.

*Variation,* 5.11d. Climb large overhang directly.

**5** 5.3. Chimney with jutting overhangs that is imposing in appearance but easy to climb.

**6** 5.5. Narrow chimney, continuation of route 5.

**7–11** 5.2–5.4. Short climbs up to and above the bench that crosses Dutchman Rampart.

**12** 5.6. Prominent upper section with overhang. Climb groove that leads behind a projecting block, surmount overhang on substantial holds.

**13** SUN SPOT, 5.7. Climb the prominent section near its right-hand corner. The hardest move is just below the top.

**14** 5.2–5.4. Short climb below and above the bench.

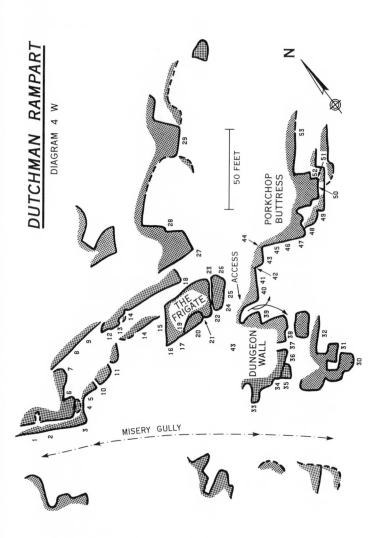

# DUTCHMAN RAMPART

DIAGRAM 4 W

50 FEET

N

MISERY GULLY

THE FRIGATE

PORKCHOP BUTTRESS

ACCESS

DUNGEON WALL

## THE FRIGATE (Diagram 4 W)

NOTE: There is no easy walk off from the top of The Frigate; descend by routes 18 or 21.

**15** POOPER, 5.9. This is the overhanging west wall of The Frigate. Climb to a small triangular niche, traverse right, then up the very strenuous hanging crack that widens into a chimney.
*Variation,* 5.12c/12d. At triangular niche continue straight up near center of face.

**16** THE STERN, 5.8. This climb leads up to the high west end of The Frigate. Start on left corner, at 10 feet move right and continue up on right corner. Finish in crack on south face.

**17** CAN-CAN, 5.5. Climb 20 feet into a niche, climb out using a high left foothold, end in chimney that splits the high west end of The Frigate.

**18** 5.3. Descent route. Short crack or step across into saddle behind The Frigate.

**19** 5.8. Thin layback crack above west end of a platform.

**20–21** 5.2. Easy cracks up to the platform and above.

**22–23** 5.2. Two chimney routes on opposite sides of The Frigate.

**24** THE JIB, 5.10b. Climb overhanging section near left corner. Join Flying Dutchman (route 25) above overhang.

**25** FLYING DUTCHMAN, 5.10a. Climb up under the right part of the southeast overhang, move left and up into a tight notch, then up a nice face to the summit block. Surmount block by a dynamic move at the southeast corner.

**26** THE BOWSPRIT, 5.8. Northeast corner of The Frigate. Start at the east corner, climb 15 feet, angling to the northeast corner (adjacent to the north chimney, route 23). Climb to base of the summit block, traverse left across the northeast side, balance onto a toehold, and retable to the top.

**27** 5.2. Buttress with mostly easy ledges on the south side.

**28** 5.4. Inside corner with crack variation.

**29** 5.4. 40-foot wall split by crack; two routes.

## DUNGEON WALL (Diagram 4 W)

**30–32** Broken rocks at base of Dungeon Wall. The dungeon has an entrance via chimney (route 31) and an escape window to the south.

**33** 5.5. Protruding section; stay on outside.

**34** 5.2. Broken chimney.

**35** 5.4. Climb easy south corner of wall, a pleasant line.

**36** DUNGEON WALL CRACK, 5.7. Climb thin crack 5 feet left of corner, near top, move left and finish in center crack. The face route avoids the right corner (route 37).
*Variation*, 5.7. Climb lower face 5 feet left of thin crack.

**37** 5.7. Corner. Start on sloping steps and follow the corner closely.

**38** 5.5. Face opposite a small tower. Start on left side of face, angle right to a small inside corner, climb to upper ledge, up crack or right corner to top.
*Variation*, 5.8. Start farther right under overhang, follow crack up and left.

**39–45** 5.7–5.11b. Climbs in the recessed section between Dungeon Wall and Porkchop Buttress. Some of these shorter climbs are more interesting that you might expect; e.g., route 42, a 5.7 inside corner, and route 40, a 5.11b face.

## PORKCHOP BUTTRESS (Diagram 4 W)

ACCESS: Ascend the bluff 100 feet north of the end of the cottage road. The first sizable outcropping encountered is Double Chimney; the next one, halfway up the bluff, is Porkchop Buttress.

**46** 5.8. South wall. Most of this wall is guarded by an overhang. Start high up the slope by the base of route 45, climb to the right to reach a high ledge, then to top.

**47** THE 100 INCH REACH, 5.11d. Start below and left of large overhang. Climb wall by placing feet on left slab, hands on wall. Move up and right, then pull through overhang.

**48** PORK LOIN, 5.7. Southeast crack and face. Climb the

crack leading to south end of a large ledge. From here climb the upper face, ending by a short, wide diagonal crack near the left corner.

**49**   JACOB'S LADDER, 5.6. Long inside corner. The steep upper section has a small overhang.

*Variation,* 5.7. Start by climbing lower narrow face just right of inside corner.

**50**   THE BONE, 5.5. Start from ledge on right side of a smooth, tapered 20-foot face. Climb the steeply angling inside corner to a moderate overhang, follow corner crack to ledge below bulging upper section, move 5 feet right, surmount bulge to reach top.

*Variation,* 5.7. From ledge below bulging upper section, climb left corner to top.

**51**   SWEAT BOX, 5.8. Climb short thin crack to platform, continue straight up on corner to overhanging block, pull directly over block.

**52**   NO EXIT, 5.7. Start climb in inside corner leading to a sloping platform, continue up to top overhang, which is passed on the left.

**53**   5.7. Shallow chimney and crack.

There is a small outcropping (not on diagram) below southeast side of Porkchop Buttress with a crack climb.

WOBBLY BLOCK, 5.5. Crack climb notable because of a wobbly block.

## DOUBLE CHIMNEY (No Diagram)

A 40-foot formation on the lower bluff, 100 feet below Porkchop Buttress. It has two towers with two chimney routes.

5.3. Stem up chimney behind the east tower.

5.2. Climb the narrower chimney of the west tower.

5.8. East side of east tower. Climb a couple of ledges, stretch far right to northeast corner and up.

SMOKE STACK, 5.9. South face of west tower. Climb center crack, starting at low point.

5.8. Climb southeast corner 15 feet, traverse right to northeast corner and up to top.

## SPLIT TOWER (See Diagram 7 W, p. 207)

ACCESS: Walk 150 feet north from base of Porkchop Buttress or descend about 150 feet from Cleopatra's Needle.

**1**   5.8. South corner overhang.

**2**   HALF MOON, 5.7. Rounded overhanging section. Start on sloping ledges, climb a jam crack in the overhang, finish on southeast corner above.

**3**   5.1. Long wide chimney which gives Split Tower it's name.

**4**   NEW MOON, 5.8. Rounded corner at right side of the long chimney. Climb close to corner to top.

**5**   MOON FACE, 5.7. An attractive face and crack route, the first 15 feet are the most difficult.

**6–8**   5.6–5.7. Short climbs below Split Tower.


## CLEO AMPHITHEATER (Diagram 5 W)

ACCESS: West Bluff Trail first emerges from the woods .35 mile from south end and overlooks the lake at a point above Cleo Amphitheater. The most convenient points of descent into the Amphitheater are directly above Cleopatra's Needle.

**1**   5.7. Wall below a small tower. Climb ledges for 20 feet, then an angling crack (crux) to a wide ledge at the base of the tower, continue on route 4.

**2**   5.1. Chimney.

**3**   5.1. Set of ledges at south end of the small tower.

**4**   5.6. From the wide ledge at base of the tower step up onto left end of a sloping shelf and climb face above.
*Variation*, 5.6. Move right on the shelf and climb overhanging jam crack.

**5**   5.8. Overhanging corner at north end of tower. Start in little chimney to the right, then hand pendulum onto corner and up.

**6**   5.5. Crack.

**7**   5.8. Short face climb leading to an inside corner.

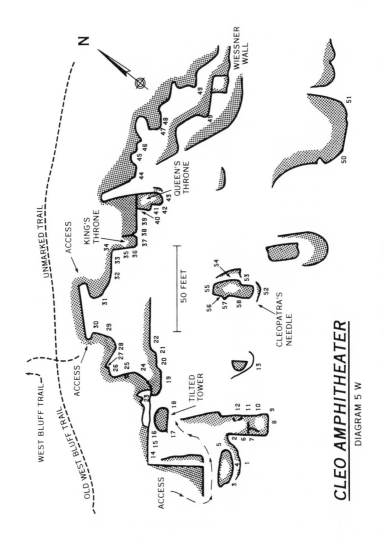

# CLEO AMPHITHEATER
### DIAGRAM 5 W

N

WEST BLUFF TRAIL

OLD WEST BLUFF TRAIL

UNMARKED TRAIL

ACCESS

ACCESS

ACCESS

ACCESS

KING'S THRONE

QUEEN'S THRONE

WIESSNER WALL

TILTED TOWER

CLEOPATRA'S NEEDLE

50 FEET

199

| 8 | 5.6. Two overhangs on southeast side. Each has a choice of climbing left or right of the overhang. |
|---|---|
| 9 | 5.8. Northeast corner. One of a group of routes (9–12) that cover the steep north face of the buttress. |
| 10 | 5.8. Crack 6 feet from northeast corner, near the top zag 3 feet to the right. |
| 11 | 5.8. Crack with layback move just left of a large niche. |
| 12 | 5.8. Stem up inside the niche, work out onto the face directly above, then climb to top. |
| 13 | 5.4. Short wall with 15 foot block at top. There are climbs on two sides. |
| 14 | 5.4. Start on dirty rock, end in one of two short chimneys 5 feet apart. |
| 15 | 5.5. The beginning of this climb is not well defined. Follow a line that crosses two small overhangs higher up. |
| 16 | PINKO, 5.7. Start in crack leading to a smooth face, balance up the face on small holds. |
| 17 | 5.3. Climb south corner of Tilted Tower. |
| 18 | TILTED TOWER, 5.9+. Climb left edge of the severely overhanging north side of tower. |
| 19 | 5.7. Climb 10 feet to a ledge, then up left crack containing a small tree. *Variation,* 5.8. Instead of the crack, ascend the rounded right-hand corner. |
| 20 | 5.4. Climb inside corner and crack, finish on left side of a pointed overhang. |
| 21 | 5.4. Crack. |
| 22 | 5.4. Inside corner. |
| 23 | 5.8. Start from ledge on wall opposite top of Tilted Tower. At north end of the ledge step right to corner (instant exposure), climb corner to top. *Variation,* 5.8–5.11a. Climb upper south face without use of corner. |
| 24 | BARNDOOR, 5.8. Follow crack to top of buttress, which is the highest point along the rim of the amphitheater. |
| 25 | 5.5. Narrow chimney. |
| 26 | COLOSTOMY, 5.7. A repulsive inside corner. |
| 27 | 5.3. Wide angle inside corner. Climb left chimney or right crack. |
| 28 | THE PLANK, 5.8. Will you sink or swim when you walk |

The Plank? Start from the crack of route 27, traverse right just above the large ceiling, move around corner to reach ascent (or sudden descent) crack.

**29** HANG DOG, 5.9. Climb to a small niche below an upper crack at north end of the large ceiling. Climb into the niche, then move left to corner and up.
*Variation,* 5.8–5.10a. From the niche, climb straight to top or slightly right into an overgrown notch.

**30** BETTER WHEN DRY, 5.7. Right side of northeast face. Climb straight up, passing diagonal crack at upper right end.

**31** CURVED WALL, 5.7. Climb 12 feet to a ledge, traverse left, then up near west end of the wall.

**32** 5.4. Jam crack.

**33** 5.4. Cracks 6 feet left of inside corner.

**34** 5.2. Inside corner.

**35** MISSING LINK, 5.8. This line is about 5 feet right of the inside corner (route 34), with the main problem between two ledges 12 feet apart.

**36** 5.5. A set of outsloping ledges.

**37** KING'S THRONE, 5.6. The higher of two promontories that jut into the north half of Cleo Amphitheater. Climb the rounded corner on a series of evenly spaced horizontal cracks and ledges.

**38** 5.5. Wide crack. At the top, continue 15 feet on north side of the highest rock of the King's Throne.

**39** 5.4. Crack.

**40** 5.3. Inside corner.

**41** QUEEN'S THRONE, 5.4. A buttress crowned by a 6-foot rock spike. Climb the clean cut inside corner/crack on comfortable ledges. An old favorite with nice exposure.

**42** BETWEEN THE QUEEN'S, 5.9. Climb on or just left of the corner. Middle section is a bit overhanging.

**43** QUEEN'S FACE, 5.8. East face of the Queen's Throne. The route keeps to the center of the narrow face. Do not use corners.

**44** JACK OF SPADES, 5.6. Crack/corner. Climb the angling crack part way, then on right side of the corner.

**45** 5.4. Chimney. Finish in left corner.

**46**  5.7. Inside corner and face.

**47**  5.7. Climb left corner to top.

**48**  5.10a. Start at small niche, climb right corner.

**49**  5.6. Corner done in two pitches. Climb lower section by left crack or on right side of the corner.

**50**  5.7. Buttress below north end of Cleo Amphitheater. Start at south corner or at overhang/crack to right of the south corner.

**51**  5.7. Northeast side of the buttress, start on the rounded corner.

## CLEOPATRA'S NEEDLE (Diagram 5 W)

**52**  5.4. Southeast side, the most popular route on Cleopatra's Needle. For esthetic reasons the climb is usually begun from a saddle on the northeast side rather than the lowest point. From the saddle cross over to the southeast side, climb (in one or two pitches) to base of the slender summit pinnacle, finish by nice face holds on southeast side or traverse around to north side just below top. NOTE: other climbs listed below generally use one of these two finishes.

**53**  5.4. Inside corner.

**54**  5.4. North ledges.

**55**  5.4. Northwest side. Ascend right side of outsloping ledges, traverse left and up to base of summit block, finish on north side, as in route 52. This is usually the down climbing route.

**56**  5.6. Inside corner/crack on left side of the southwest rib.

**57**  5.7. Southwest rib. Climb bottom overhang to get onto outside of the rib. Follow rib to ledge at base of summit block, move left and finish on northwest face of block.

**58**  5.4. Two cracks to the right of the southeast rib.
*Variation*, 5.5. Climb using only the right crack.

## TURK'S HEAD (Diagram 6 W)

ACCESS: Starting where the West Bluff Trail overlooks Cleopatra's Needle, follow an unmarked path 200 feet north, turn right down the bluff through a gully system on the north side of

Turk's Head. Or use the access routes into Cleo Amphitheater. Wiessner Wall is 150 feet north of Cleopatra's Needle.

**1** THE WASP, 5.7. Roof at south end of Wiessner Wall. Ascend ledges on the inner wall beneath the roof, traverse right (around corner) onto outer wall, ascend a jam crack to ledge.

**2** FRITZ, 5.7. Start in moderate crack 15 feet north of the roof, climb crack 15 feet, then move 5 feet left and climb a thin face crack to ledge.

**3** STINGER, 5.8. Climb crack leading to niche, then climb on outside just left of the niche to reach exit crack ending at ledge above.

**4** WIESSNER CHIMNEY, 5.4. Awkward narrow chimney that will seem harder if you don't find the right combination. Climb to base of slab, traverse left to north end of ledge.

**5** JUST ANOTHER PRETTY FACE, 5.11a. Climb center of face on small holds to base of slab.
*Variation*, 5.9. Same start, but move left and climb near edge of face close to Wiessner Chimney (route 4).

The following three climbs start from the ledge mentioned in routes 1–4.

**6** 5.4. From ledge, climb into shallow niche with sloping floor, continue up chockstone crack.

**7** 5.2. Wide crack above north end of ledge. There may be loose rock in the crack, but the chief concern is likely to be wasp nests.

**8** WIESSNER FACE, 5.7. A pretty face climb on north part of the wall. From north end of ledge climb onto a bulge at base of the smooth upper face, then climb a set of horizontal cracks to top of the wall.
*Variation*, 5.7. Start from base of slab at top of Wiessner Chimney (route 4). Climb on or near corner for 15 feet, continue on Wiessner face.

**9** 5.2. Inside corner.

**10** TURK'S HEAD, 5.5 (southeast corner). Climb corner to overhang, finish on south side. Descend on south side or jump down from a short V-chimney on west side.

Cleopatra's Needle (diagram 5 W). Climbers: B. Plumley, E. Clark, D. Plumley, J. Hawkes. Photo: Harold Plumley.

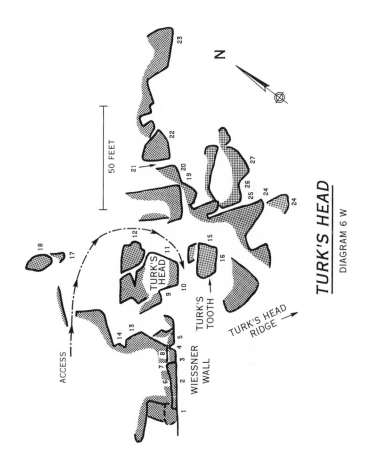

# *TURK'S HEAD*

DIAGRAM 6 W

N

50 FEET

ACCESS

TURK'S HEAD

WIESSNER WALL

TURK'S TOOTH

TURK'S HEAD RIDGE

205

**11** 5.6. Northeast ledges and overhang. Climb northeast side of Turk's Head to ledge beneath the wide overhang, reach up into central notch and mantle onto ledge above the overhang. Walk around to south side for easiest way to top.

*Variation,* 5.6. Surmount overhang by crawling onto shelf at north end. No one has ever looked good doing this.

**12** 5.7. Rib with overhang. Tackle the overhang from either side.

**13** 5.11b. Climb center of face.

**14** 5.2. Adjacent chimneys behind Turk's Head.

**15** TURK'S TOOTH, 5.2. A tower just below Turk's Head. The northeast side of this tower is a pleasant ledge climb. Descend on the west side (facing Turk's Head).

**16** A POINT OF BALANCE, 5.8. Overhang/chimney. Balance onto the point of a large flake from which the overhang can be reached if you're tall enough. Move left and up into the hanging chimney that breaches the overhang.

**17** 5.4. Small tower. Climb east corner in two sections, descend south crack.

**18** 5.5. North face of the small tower.

**19** 5.6. Crack/overhang. Climb left-slanting crack 15 feet, then up the overhang right of the crack.

*Variation,* 5.7. Continue up the crack. Surprisingly, this turns out to be harder than doing the overhang.

**20** 5.7. Start at the same point as route 19, work right beneath the corner overhang, reach high and feel for hold on the next ledge, surmount overhang, proceed on the wall and ledges above.

**21** 5.2. Chimney.

**22** 5.5. Tower. Start on northeast side, or start near south corner and angle right across southeast face. Mantle left onto ledge 25 feet up, traverse right to finish on northeast side.

**23** 5.7. Climb 15 feet at east corner, traverse 5 feet left on a ledge, then up south side. The summit band essentially ends with this buttress.

**24** 5.7. Corner. Climb uppermost section obstructed by a pine tree on north side.

**25** GREEN SLIME, 5.10b. A sheer lichen-encrusted wall

with a hanging crack. Climb 10 feet straight up to the beginning of the crack. At the crux, stem out to the right and get a grip using a thumb jam in the narrowest part of the crack.

**26**  5.5. Climb face and upper corner, staying a few feet right of the chimney.

**27**  5.8. Face leading to V-chimney. It takes close examination to find the holds.

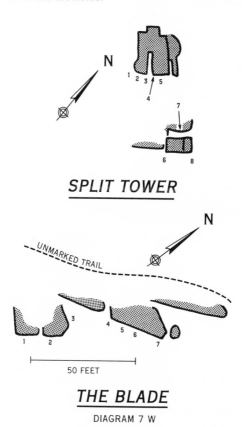

## SPLIT TOWER

## THE BLADE

DIAGRAM 7 W

## THE BLADE (Diagram 7 W)

ACCESS: From the top of the bluff above Turk's Head, follow an unmarked path that gradually descends to the north. At 300 feet it passes above The Blade.

1    5.3. Overhang to left of central chimney.
2    5.2. Chimney and adjacent rock.
3    5.7. Crack climbed by layback and jamming.
4    5.4. South corner of the main wall.
5    5.6. Climb crack holding a small pine tree, continue straight up over top overhang.
6    DEAR ABBEY, 5.8. Climb on small ledges to a niche at the center of the wall, step up into a thin crack, climb crack to top.
7    THE BLADE, 5.6. An acute-angled northeast corner. Step onto the corner from a block on the north side, continue on or near corner to top.
     *Variation*, 5.7. Finish via a thin crack 5 feet left of corner.

## TURK'S HEAD RIDGE (No Diagram)

ACCESS: Tumbled Rocks Trail, 350 feet north of the cottages. Ascend bluff 200 feet to lowest outcropping visible above.

FIRST PITCH is a small tower with the following climbs.

5.2. Climb the wide crack to northeast side of tower. Descend the south crack (easiest), southwest corner, or northwest corner.
5.9. Northeast side just left of the wide crack.
5.5. Southeast corner. Mount a block beneath corner overhang, get around the overhang on the center face.

Forty feet south of the small tower is a short wall with a couple of climbs leading to Second Pitch platform.

5.6. 20-foot overhanging, dirty, inside corner.
5.8. Narrow face 10 feet left of inside corner. Climb right side on widely spaced ledges.

**SECOND PITCH**, a 30-foot wall.

> 5.6. Starting from a detached platform, climb small ledges on north half of the wall.
>
> PINCH FINGER, 5.8. A left-angling crack in the smooth south part of the wall.

**THIRD PITCH**, a 15-foot wall.

> 5.2. Climb the obvious central crack or chimney on the left.

**FOURTH PITCH**, a narrow, ridge-like section 40 feet high.

> 5.2. Wide crack starting behind a tree on southeast side. Climb the crack 25 feet, finish on southeast ledges.
> *Variation*, 5.4. Start in the crack, about 10 feet up traverse right to east corner and climb the corner.
> 5.4. Narrow corner on south side, separated from main ridge by sloping V-chimney.
> 5.9. Crack in the steep north wall of the ridge. Climb the crack through a niche. There is a delicate layback just above the niche. When crack ends, move left to east corner.

**FIFTH PITCH**, a 20-foot step.

> 5.5. Southeast corner.
> 5.4. Climb the diagonal crack to the northeast corner.
> 5.2. Walk around south side for other variations.

**SIXTH PITCH**: Scramble up the crest of the ridge to platform at base of Turk's Tooth.

> 5.4–5.5. On south flank of the ridge there is a niche with two cracks radiating upward. Either crack may be followed.

# Prospect Point Towers

These towers form a ridge on the middle third of the bluff below Prospect Point.

ACCESS: Take Tumbled Rocks Trail north to the 150 Foot Boulderfield. Ascend the boulders, or a faint path in the trees to the south, to the base of the first tower. Several large blocks, with short overhanging chimneys between them, are encountered a little below the first tower.

## FIRST TOWER (Diagram 8 W)

**1**    5.6. 25-foot wall at base of First Tower.

**2**    5.4. Climb northeast corner of 15-foot tower. Southwest side is best way off.

## SUN-TOP TOWER (Diagram 8 W)

**3**    CAN'T CAN'T, 5.11a. Start near south corner, climb easily to ledge at 15 feet, traverse left to the pointed nose, where a chorus-line kick can be employed to achieve a stemming position in the wide inside corner. Work up inside corner, go left onto nose, or continue straight up.

**4**    THE SUCKER, 5.7. Climb a short wall with crack leading to ledge at base of V-chimney, climb chimney to top. *Variation,* 5.5. Climb to the ledge at south corner, move right to chimney and up.

**5**    MOON BEAM, 5.11b/11c. Climb difficult face between The Sucker (route 4) and Sun-Top (route 6). A long reach makes the climb easier.

**6**    SUN-TOP, 5.8. Crack/overhang behind a pine tree. Named to commemorate the day this lecherous tree snagged the brief garment worn by a female climber. Climb to ledge below the overhang, work up to reach a good horizontal crack on the left, then bring feet up high while leaning left and reach for handhold in exit crack, climb to top.

**7**    MAY FLY, 5.7. Overhang/crack. Start directly below

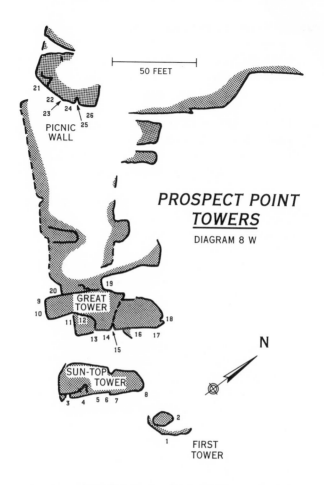

PROSPECT POINT
*TOWERS*

DIAGRAM 8 W

N

upper, small inside corner of route 8, 10 feet right of Sun-Top (route 6). Climb into niche, up right past overhang to ledge at 20 feet, then traverse left 6 feet to a crack, follow crack to top.

*Variation,* MAY FLY DIRECT, 5.11d. Same start. From niche, move left to overhanging flake, climb up and right to ledge. Finish in upper May Fly crack.

**8** 5.7. Northeast ridge. Climb sloping ledges to a small inside corner near the top, on east side of the ridge. Do one hard move to reach platform above.

## GREAT TOWER (Diagram 8 W)

DESCENT ROUTE: From the top of Great Tower, drop down a short wall behind the east high point, contour west until the gully on the south side of the ridge is reached (near Picnic Wall).

**9** ROCK GARDEN, 5.7. Climb southwest corner with a small overhanging section near the top.

**10** GARDEN PATH, 5.7. Climb lower overhang and face on south side of Great Tower on sharp holds typical of south exposures.

*Variation,* MOON ROCK, 5.8. Same start. Climb up and right to south corner, follow corner to top.

**11** THE GREAT CRACK, 5.6. This is the classic climb on the Great Tower. Inside corner/crack on east face just left of the large overhang. The route goes over several ledges that divide it into short sections.

**12** STEAK SAUCE, 5.12c. Large overhang with crack. The route was originally rated A1 (aid route). Note: No aid routes in book.

**13** 5.7. Climb corner at north end of the overhang, continue in crack above.

*Variation,* MOON WALK, 5.10a. Same start, climb corner to overhang. Then hand traverse left to point of overhang on holds just above the overhang, pull up and continue to top.

**14** 5.8. Thin crack in the face just south of the chimney (route 15).

**15** 5.4. Chimney.

**16** CRACKER BARREL, 5.7. Climb the flake edge crack and continue straight up a short face to a large platform. From here ledges and short walls lead to the top of the tower.

**17** SLY CORNER, 5.8. Northeast corner. Climb, staying left of the corner to a ledge underneath overhang, move left onto face and up to large platform.

**18** 5.7. Climb wide crack to ledge under overhang. Step on block beneath overhang and work somewhat right to reach vertical holds that lead to the large platform above.

**19** 5.4. North chimney, dirty, long and exposed.

**20**     5.2. South chimney, an alpine-like route for ascent or descent.

## PICNIC WALL (Diagram 8 W)

**21**     BASKET, 5.6. Climb into a niche, traverse out around right corner, continue to top.

**22**     NO PICNIC, 5.9. Here is the climb to stretch you out. Secure a beautiful handhold that is just out of reach from the ground, reach far up to the right for the second (not the first) little triangular pocket, continue climbing on widely spaced holds to the overhang above, which should now seem easy.

**23**     TRACK CRACKS, 5.8. Climb the parallel cracks, using twin jam holds at the crux 12 feet up.

**24**     5.9. Climb face close to right corner.

**25**     5.5. Chimney, finish on left corner.

**26**     5.11b. Boulder problem.

## Prospect Point Rampart

ACCESS: Prospect Point is .5 mile from the south end of the West Bluff Trail. Climbs near Prospect Point are accessible by walking down around the south end of the rampart. Climbs farther north can be reached by descending the Great Chimney or Lost Face access gully. When approaching the area from below, ascend south edge of the 500 Foot Boulderfield.

## PROSPECT POINT to BIG TOE (Diagram 9 W)

Below the south side of Prospect Point there are a number of short routes that offer convenient climbing near the trail.

**I**     5.8. Corner. Start from lowest point and climb corner without use of blocks on left.
      5.11d. Narrow face right of corner in route 1. Avoid using holds near or on corner.

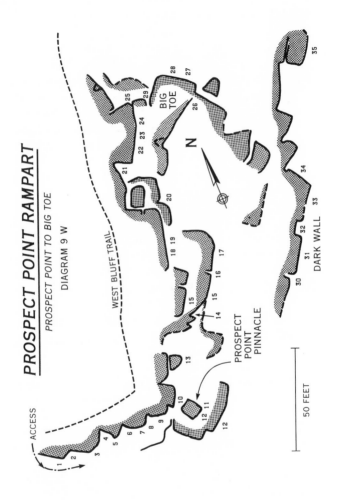

# PROSPECT POINT RAMPART

*PROSPECT POINT TO BIG TOE*

DIAGRAM 9 W

WEST BLUFF TRAIL

ACCESS

N

BIG TOE

PROSPECT POINT PINNACLE

DARK WALL

50 FEET

**2**    5.6. Awkward crack.

**3**    5.7. Climb crack right of corner.
*Variation*, 5.6. Start in crack a few feet farther right.

**4**    5.4. Inside corner.

**5**    5.7. Slightly overhanging corner.

**6**    5.8. Climb shallow inside corner, finish in crack.

**7**    5.9. Climb the lower bulging wall to crack. Follow crack to top.

**8**    5.7. Inside corner.

**9**    5.10a. Overhang with two cracks above.

**10**    PROSPECT POINT PINNACLE I, 5.2. This small tower is just off the top of the bluff. Start from the saddle between pinnacle and bluff and climb northwest side.

**11**    PINNACLE ARETE, 5.10b. Climb the very sharp south corner.

**12**    PROSPECT POINT PINNACLE II, 5.8. Start in crack on short wall, below southeast side of the Pinnacle. Climb the wall to platform that supports the tower, up southeast side to a sloping ledge, mantle on south side to reach top.
*Variation*, 5.9. From first ledge (8 feet up), climb thin crack starting at west end of ledge.

**13**    5.8. Corner of a small tower.

**14**    5.6. Inside corner with crack.

**15**    5.6. Start at two cracks 3 feet apart, climb either, or both, to platform 25 feet up, ascend ledges and finish on upper wall.

**16–17**    5.4. Broken wall with ledges, mixed climbing and scrambling.

**18**    5.6. Crack leading to V-niche.

**19**    5.8. Climb upper wall through two small niches, end with a short crack that angles to the right.

**20**    5.8. Short slabby inside corner leading to a chimney complex.

**21**    5.4. V-chimney.

**22**    5.7. Start up a thin crack, finish a bit left in chimney with overhanging capstones.

**23**    WIDULE 7, 5.9. Start with a bucket hold on first ledge (4 feet north of route 22), mount the ledge and continue straight to top.

**24**    5.9. Overhanging section of lower wall. Start in short

Prospect Point Pinnacle II (diagram 9 W, route 12). Climber: Jack Fletcher. Photo: Sven Olof Swartling.

crack, at 6 feet step right onto a ledge, then work up using a jam hold in the flaring crack above.

**25**    THE HEEL, 5.11a. Northeast corner. Climb corner with an interesting heel hook.

**26**    BIG TOE, 5.2. Start behind a cobra-head-shaped tower, climb near east corner of Big Toe onto the large sloping platform.

**27**    5.9. Crack on northeast side of Big Toe.

**28**    5.7. Flake route 5 feet right of route 27.
*Variation*, 5.8. Climb first 8 feet directly.

**29**    5.2. Short chimney leading onto Big Toe.

## DARK WALL (Diagram 9 W)

**30**    5.2. Chimney.

**31**    5.6. Wall with ledge halfway up, climb to south end of ledge, then up left to top.

**32**    5.3. Wide chimney.

**33**    SOUL FOOD, 5.9. Slightly overhanging face. Climb onto ledge at 10 feet, then up thin crack to top.

**34**    5.6. Nondescript wall facing northeast.

**35**    5.7. Face of the tower at north end of the Dark Wall.

## BIG TOE to GREAT CHIMNEY (Diagram 10 W)

Some of these routes are on the lower half of the cliff, others on the upper half. Use various combinations to form complete ascents. Ledges separating lower and upper routes are labeled **DD** to **GG** on the diagram.

**36**    5.10b. Start below a pointed nose 20 feet up. Climb to top of the nose, then up crack to upper ledge **DD.**
*Variation,* 5.9. Climb 10 feet on rib below the slab, and step left and up delicate, lichen-covered rock to ledge level with top of the nose.

**37**    5.6. Chimney on north side of the pointed nose.

**38**    GRAND ILLUSION, 5.9. Crack/overhang above ledge **DD.** Climb left-slanting crack toward a notch in the upper

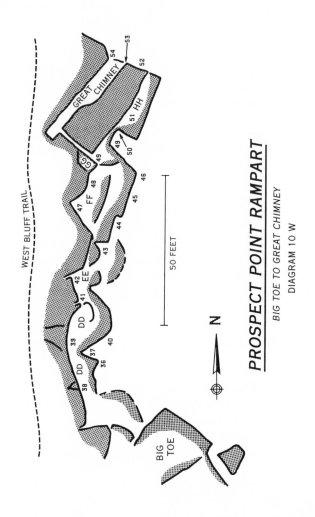

## PROSPECT POINT RAMPART

*BIG TOE TO GREAT CHIMNEY*

DIAGRAM 10 W

N

50 FEET

wall. Don't go into the notch; traverse left beneath the overhang and climb crack in overhang to top.

**39** 5.2. A couple of steps lead to a recessed section in the upper wall. This is more or less an escape route from ledge **DD.**

**40** 5.4. Start in adjacent chimney (route 37), cross north onto first large ledge and into a small inside corner, scramble up to ledge **EE.**

**41** 5.8. Crack and notch just north of a corner on the upper wall. Reach the crack from ledge **EE** below or by traversing north on ledge **DD.**

**42** 5.5. Inside corner with chimney above north end of ledge **EE.**

**43** 5.4. Climb in V-chimney, then continue to the right up slabby rock to reach ledge **FF.**

**44** 5.7. Climb inside corner and cracks on 30-foot lower wall.

**45** ICARUS, 5.11d. Climb face with wide stems and long reaches to ledge **FF.**

**46** 5.4. Start on the outside corner and climb right into a 20-foot crack. Pass 6-foot arrowhead flake and step onto the ledge above, go left around the corner, and scramble to ledge **FF.**

**47** 5.4. Inside corner above south end of ledge **FF.**
*Variation,* 5.8. Overhanging crack just left of inside corner.

**48** 5.7. From north end of ledge **FF,** climb short wall to small platform **GG,** 15 feet below the top. Finish on south wall.

**49** DOUBLE JEOPARDY, 5.6. This chimney provides a continuous ascent of the entire wall. Start in south inside corner of rectangular recessed section, climb chimney past a couple of overhanging chockstones to platform **GG,** then to top.

**50** STUCK KNEE, 5.7. Start in north inside corner of the recessed section, climb 15 feet to first ledge, then up crack to base of a narrow chimney. Climb chimney (crux) to ledge above, finish in 12-foot inside corner or on easy ledges on the left.

**51** BIVOUAC LEDGE, 5.12b a.k.a. DANCE OF THE GHOST PSAMEAD, 5.12b. Start by climbing onto the

Son of Great Chimney (diagram 10 W, route 52). Climber: Alex Andrews. Photo: Sven Olof Swartling.

point of a boulder resting on ledge **HH.** Climb wall above, following a crack past overhang to the bivouac ledge, then up a wider crack at north end of the ledge.

**52** SON OF GREAT CHIMNEY, 5.11a. A hideous promontory, suggestive of The End on the East Bluff. From ledge **HH,** cross over to northeast corner of the promontory, go around corner and up north wall to a cramped ledge. Then up overhanging crack (crux) a few feet to handholds at same level as Bivouac Ledge (to which escape is possible). Traverse right and grasp a welcome rock prong at northwest corner, climb corner to top.

**53** MATCH THE SNATCH, 5.12a/12b. Start on face near left corner, 15 feet above base of Great Chimney. Climb up and left to corner, pass overhang, then move up right for the snatch. Finish on Son of Great Chimney (route 52).

**54** GREAT CHIMNEY, 5.3. A frequently used access route. There is a steep part at the bottom that is tricky.

## GREAT CHIMNEY to LOST FACE (Diagram II W)

**55** COUP D'ÉTAT, 5.11b. Start in zigzagging crack just left of Handle With Care (route 56). Continue straight up textured rock in thin crack.

**56** HANDLE WITH CARE, 5.5. Climb the flaky crack to a platform, continue in a short chimney to top.

**57** 5.8. Start on face near chimney (route 58), move left to a ledge and follow crack to platform above.

**58** 5.6. Narrow chimney. Staying outside the chimney provides better climbing.

**59** 5.6. Crack.

**60** THE GOOD, THE BAD, AND THE JACKED, 5.12a. Start 3 feet right of corner on left edge of huge block. Climb past fixed pin and enjoy dynamic move at the top.

**61** CRACKER JACK, 5.8. Climb obvious 30-foot crack to top of huge block. Climb 10 feet (crux) to next ledge, then continue more easily to top of wall.

**62** MILKING THE BULL, 5.12c. Face with thin cracks and overhang at top.

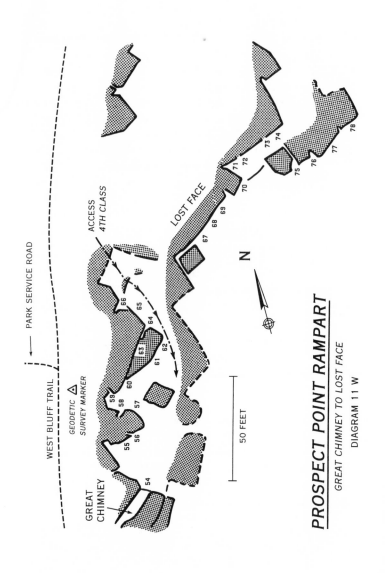

# PROSPECT POINT RAMPART

GREAT CHIMNEY TO LOST FACE

DIAGRAM 11 W

**63** WILD WEST HOMO, 5.11a. Climb overhanging face 10 to 15 feet right of The Good, The Bad, and The Jacked (route 60).

**64** 5.4. Narrow chimney.

**65** WHIPPING BOY, 5.10c. Climb cracks.

**66** 5.4. Inside corner with crack.

**67** LOST FACE, 5.6. Longest climb on the West Bluff. Start on slanting ledge, climb crack system that leads fairly directly into niche in the center of the face. Climb inside corner of niche, then ledges, ending at large ledge on south side of summit boulder.

*Variation,* LOST FACE OVERHANG I, 5.8. Before reaching niche, traverse left and climb right side of overhang 6 feet south of niche.

*Variation,* LOST FACE OVERHANG II, 5.8. Before reaching niche, traverse left under overhang, surmount it by a crack 12 feet south of niche, continue straight up to large ledge.

**68** 5.7. Thin crack that splits 15 feet up. Left crack joins Lost Face (route 67); right crack ends at a walk off halfway up north edge of the face.

**69** IBEX, 5.11a. Smooth section of the face between the crack (route 68) and north edge. The route continues onto a narrow bulge 40 feet up.

**70** DELICATE MOVES, 5.8. Separate steep slab with delicate moves, especially on upper part near north edge.

**71** 5.4. Chimney.

**72** 5.8. Start in niche, ascend overhang and crack above.

**73** 5.7. Crack at north end of small overhang.

**74** 5.2. Crack. Used as access route.

**75–78** 5.5–5.7. Short chimneys and faces.

## RECLINING TOWER (Diagram 12 W)

ACCESS: Reclining Tower and Dead Tree Wall are respectively 175 and 425 feet north of the geodetic marker on the West Bluff Trail. There is an access gully leading down from the trail just south of each formation.

Lost Face Overhang II (diagram 11 W, route 67).
Climber: Marcus Hall. Photo: Sven Olof Swartling.

| | |
|---|---|
| **1** | 5.2. Broken ledges. |
| **2** | 5.6. Start under overhang, continue in crack above. |
| **3** | 5.7. South side of corner. |
| **4** | X-RATED, 5.10a. Start near northeast corner, climb 8 feet left to flake under overhang, move right toward corner, reach up for a small projection and retable. Continue on corner to top. |
| **5** | 5.7. Climb east corner to base of tower, balance up left onto south corner of the tower. Climb corner to top, step over gap and climb short wall above. |
| **6** | 5.7. Climb crack and V-chimney 25 feet onto right-hand ledge, retable to next ledge. Continue up and right to third ledge (crux) and top. |
| **7** | 5.6. Two large flakes. Climb north edge of the flakes, then join route 6. |
| **8** | 5.4. Chimney on south side of Reclining Tower. There is one point where one can squeeze behind the tower to reach the north side (route 12). |
| **9** | PINE TREE CRACK, 5.8. Start in corner. Climb crack and overhang to pine tree 15 feet up. |
| **10** | RECLINING TOWER ARETE, 5.11d. Climb lower difficult corner to platform at 20 feet. Continue on arete (5.6) in two stages to top of Tower. *Variation,* 5.6. Start on route 12, at 20 feet traverse left to platform and continue as above. |
| **11** | SOLAR WIND, 5.11c. Climb short face to platform just left of route 12. |
| **12** | 5.6. North side of Reclining Tower. Climb inside corner and deep awkward crack to top of the tower. |

## DEAD TREE WALL (Diagram 12 W)

| | |
|---|---|
| **13–15** | Minor summit rocks south of Dead Tree Wall. |
| **16** | 5.6. Short face climb. |
| **17** | 5.6. Inside corner. |
| **18** | AMAZING GRACE, 5.9. Climb onto detached block below first overhang, pass it on right with a nice balance move, pass the upper overhang on left. *Variation,* 5.12a. Climb upper overhang directly. |
| **19** | DEFEAT OF THE BOYS, 5.11c. Climb, following the |

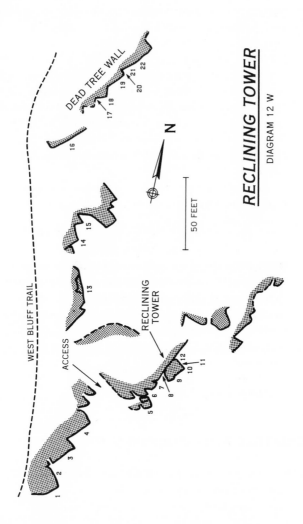

WEST BLUFF TRAIL

DEAD TREE WALL

ACCESS

RECLINING TOWER

N

50 FEET

*RECLINING TOWER*

DIAGRAM 12 W

shallow dihedral and tight seam 4 to 6 feet left of Dead Tree Climb (route 20).

**20** DEAD TREE CLIMB, 5.8. Start in inside corner, continue in wide crack containing an old tree stump. The overhang below the stump is the crux.

**21** THE CMC LIVES, 5.11c. Face and overhang between Dead Tree Climb (route 20) and Tardis (route 22).

**22** TARDIS, 5.10b. Thin crack 10 feet north of Dead Tree Climb (route 20).

*Variation,* 5.9. Start farther right (north), traverse into crack system at 12 feet.

## CAVE ROCKS RAMPART (Diagram 13 W)

**1** 5.0. Access gully.

**2** 5.7. Broken wall with overhangs. There is some loose rock.

**3** 5.8. Corner.

**4** 5.4. Crack.

**5** 5.5. Climb short chimney to notch containing tree, continue up on the outside, left or right of the notch.

**6** THE CLAMSHELL, 5.6. Climb corner crack on south side of chimney (route 7) to a pair of sharp-edged blocks that cover the chimney; continue behind the upper block or crawl between the two. Four feet below top of the upper block, step over (south) to a platform and finish on wall above.

**7** 5.2. Large chimney.

**8** 5.5. Climb on south side of corner for 15 feet, move around corner and climb to top.

**9** SOUTH ENCLOSURE, 5.7. Climb inside the enclosure by stemming or laybacking.

**10** NORTH ENCLOSURE, 5.6. Climb inside the enclosure facing north, using left-hand crack for layback.

**11–13** 5.3–5.6. Short climbs.

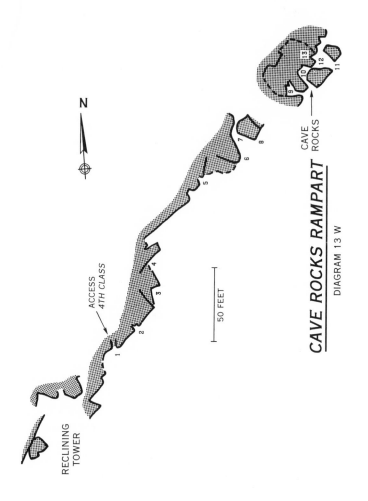

N

RECLINING TOWER

ACCESS
4TH CLASS

50 FEET

CAVE ROCKS

## *CAVE ROCKS RAMPART*

DIAGRAM 13 W

# HANGMAN TOWERS (No Diagram)

There are scattered rocks which deserve some mention 100 to 500 feet north of Dead Tree Wall. The descriptions start at the lower level and proceed upward.

The lowest climbs are located by reference to The Turtle, a landmark boulder which can be reached from Tumbled Rocks Trail (see West Bluff approaches). From The Turtle ascend 100 feet to The Hangman, roughly midlevel on the bluff.

> THE HANGMAN, 5.7. Deep inside corner and crack with overhang. Where the crack runs through the overhang it appears possible to hang by one's head. To avoid the possibility, use an incredibly dirty chockstone.
>
> 5.6. Southeast side of The Hangman. The climb starts from a block.

TWIN RIDGE. From The Hangman walk up (slightly south) 150 feet to the base of Twin Ridge. The north ridge starts at a lower level and is separated from the south ridge by a narrow gully.

> NORTH TWIN RIDGE, 5.4. Four or five short pitches, starting with two towers and a short wall that leads to a back-sloping platform (lunch spot) about 100 feet below the summit.
>
> SOUTH TWIN RIDGE, 5.6. The base of the south ridge is a pair of detached blocks. Chimney up behind the lower block (tricky start) to base of an imposing section. Continue on south side.
>
> NOWHERE LEDGE, 5.10a. Step onto a diagonal ledge below the imposing section of the south ridge, move right and climb near northeast corner to platform above.
>
> ONCE IS ENOUGH, 5.9. North side of the south ridge. Climb a cul-de-sac chimney into a hanging inside corner, then up corner to top.
>
> KNOBBY PILLAR, 5.4–5.8. A narrow tower 50 feet southwest of the lunch spot on North Twin Ridge. Start at the south corner or climb the more difficult northeast overhang and corner.

BIRD BATH TOWER, 5.8. A 25-foot tower 60 feet south of the upper part of Twin Ridge. Climb northeast side, using the seemingly innocuous ledge halfway up.

THE BEAST. From the base of Twin Ridge go south 100 feet, crossing a low rock ridge with an extended southeast face. The Beast is a 15-foot block sitting on a pedestal.
5.4. Climb the obvious inside corner on the east side of the pedestal, then climb the northeast corner of the block.
5.5–5.7. A compact group of towers 40 feet south of The Beast with three routes.

GO-GO TOWER is 70 feet north of the lunch spot on Twin Ridge.
GO-GO, 5.7. Southeast corner with an interesting layback and dynamic moves.
5.7. Southeast face.
GOING, GOING, GONE, 5.9. Overhanging ledges on east side.
*Variation,* 5.9. Between second and third ledge, climb northeast corner.

From Go-Go Tower follow a faint path angling down and north to a band of rocks 80 feet long. The area is about a third of the way down the bluff, 200 feet north of the Twin Ridge.

SHARK'S TOOTH, 5.7. Tower at upper (south) end of the band. Climb V-chimney that starts above the first ledge. Avoid the little platform on north side of the chimney.
5.8. Northeast corner; avoid ledge on left.
THE PORPOISE, 5.4. A narrow fin-shaped structure at the lower (north) end of the band, easily climbed on the ridge, which is more solid that it appears.
5.7. North side of The Porpoise. Difficulty depends on how resolutely one stays on the face.
5.8. The center section of the band consists of two shape-

less buttresses. Climb south buttress on south corner or southeast face.

NERVES, 5.7. Climb southeast corner of north buttress.


## TREE TOWER (Diagram 14 W)

ACCESS: On the West Bluff Trail, about two-thirds of the way to the north end of the lake, there is a small boulderfield that reaches almost to the trail. Tree Tower is 200 feet north of the boulderfield. The access gully is a little south of Tree Tower.

**1**   TREE TOWER, 5.7. The traditional route on the tower. Start near lowest point, climb ledges on east ridge to an inside corner on northeast side. Climb this interesting inside corner with a peculiar rock splinter. Descend by route 3.

**2**   5.2. Southeast side, broken by very favorable vertical holds.

**3**   5.2. Flake on south side used as descent route.

**4**   BOWLER'S GRIP, 5.8. Climb the northwest side, using (if possible) the two finger holes below the upper horizontal crack.

**5**   5.8. North side. Start just left of obtuse north corner, climb up and left onto block, then up crack to the pine tree.

**6**   TOON TOWN, 5.11c/11d. Climb lower face just left of obtuse corner to ledge, continue on upper face without using block on left (routes 5 and 6 cross on the ledge).

**7**   5.8. Climb just left of small overhang.

**8**   5.8. This climb goes directly up the small overhang.

**9**   5.7. Climb corner adjacent to recess.

**10**   5.4. Ledges adjacent to the corner on north side of recess.

**11–16**   5.2–5.6. Chimneys and corners.

**17**   5.6. Layback crack.

**18**   FLYING INDIAN, 5.7. Climb crack, using mostly finger and toe jams. Routes 17 and 18 are only a couple of feet apart; they are most interesting if kept separate.

**19**   SERENDIPITY, 5.11b/11c. Face with thin holds and high steps.

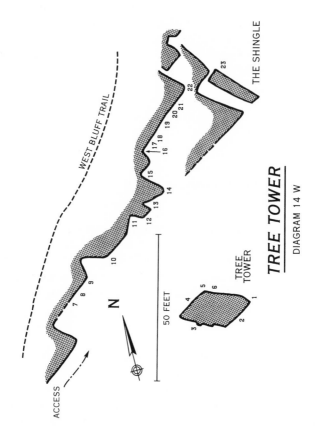

## *TREE TOWER*

DIAGRAM 14 W

WEST BLUFF TRAIL

THE SHINGLE

TREE TOWER

ACCESS

N

50 FEET

**20** TROUBLE, 5.9. Face with thin crack. Avoid moving right near the top.

**21** NO TROUBLE, 5.8. Another thin crack, this one passing small overhang.

**22** KOALA BEAR, 5.11a. Shinny up corner, using holds on both sides.

**23** THE SHINGLE, 5.10a. A narrow vertical formation below the main wall. Climb northwest corner, adjacent to gap at west end.

## No Diagram

A 30-foot-high summit wall 150 feet south of Tree Tower projects over the boulderfield, forming a sharp corner of clear rock.

DER SCHNOZZEL, 5.8. Start on right side of the corner or from boulder on left side. Step up onto the corner, climb from ledge to ledge until a rock divot on right side is reached. Please use carefully and replace for next climber.

CAKE WALK, 5.9. Start on south side of the corner, climb the smooth face to a crack, then up crack to top.

5.4–5.6. Inside corner and face climbs on wall 20 to 40 feet south of Cake Walk.

## TYROLEAN TOWER (No Diagram)

ACCESS: Tyrolean Tower is 200 feet north of Tree Tower below an elevated vantage point along the crest of the bluff. There is a short rise in the trail when approaching from the south. Descend 100 feet to base of tower.

5.2. Easy chimney on the south side leading to a gap behind the 20-foot summit block.

5.10d. Face just right of easy chimney, also leading to gap behind summit block.

5.6. Start 15 feet right of the easy chimney, climb crack up and left into gap behind the summit block.

*Variation,* 5.6. Climb part way up the crack, then traverse right and climb up to north platform (level with gap behind).

THE GAP, 5.8. Start in gap on southwest side of the summit block. Climb thin crack for 5 feet, then move right to south corner and follow corner to top.

*Variation,* 5.9. Continue straight up above the thin crack.

TYROLEAN TOWER, 5.10d. Start at base of tower and climb the southeast corner and overhang to top.

FREE AT LAST, 5.11a. Start on northeast side at base of tower, climb the lower rounded section to a ledge, continue in crack to north platform, finish on north wall of summit block.

The wall immediately southwest of Tyrolean Tower has three nice routes.

RIGHT EDGE, 5.7. Climb broken rock near right edge of wall to a ledge, continue on southeast corner.

LONE PINE DIAGONAL, 5.8. Start 8 feet left of Right Edge, climb diagonal crack past small pine tree. Continue, following crack when it turns straight up (about two-thirds of the way up).

LAST CRACK, 5.10c. Left thin crack in wall.

There is a summit buttress 500 feet north of Tyrolean Tower. It is not visible from the trail; walk about 25 feet east to reach the top.

PEARLY GATE, 5.9. Obvious inside corner on east side of the buttress.

5.7. North side of buttress. Climb crack up and left to corner. Move around corner and finish on the east face with a creaking flake.

5.11a. North side of buttress. Start in same crack, but continue up north face to top.

ARM POWER, 5.11d. South corner. Start climb just left of corner. Climb face and overhang straight to top.

5.7. South side of buttress. Climb left-angling crack, pass overhang on left.

There is another outcropping 150 feet south of Pearly Gate, at a lower level.

> INCH WORM, 5.8. Climb a shallow inside corner on southeast side past north end of overhang.

## BY GULLY (No Diagram)

ACCESS: From the north end of the West Bluff Trail, walk .25 mile to the head of a large dirt gully with an outcropping on the north side, 100 feet down. There are two buttresses.

> 5.6. South corner of south buttress, adjacent to the gully. Start at slightly overhanging corner, continue in crack and ledge system to top.
> PEE-WEE'S INNOCENT, 5.12a. Overhanging southeast face of buttress. Climb center of face.
> ROCK DIVOT, 5.9. North-facing wall of south buttress. Climb thin crack just right (west) of corner. A small rock divot hides one of the good holds.
> *Variation,* 5.9. Corner left of crack.
> USE YOUR FEET, 5.8. North-facing wall of south buttress. Climb into obvious niche, continue above in cracks leading right or left of nose.
> MOSS BE GONE, 5.9. Thin crack 4 feet right of niche noted in previous climb.
> 5.6. South side of north buttress. Inside corner with crack.
> 5.10b. Southeast corner of north buttress. Climb as close to corner as possible.
> ARE WE HAVING FUN YET, 5.10d. Southeast face of north buttress. Climb slightly overhanging face, starting directly below crack in upper part of face. Finish in upper crack.
> 5.4. Inside corner a couple of feet farther right (north).

# HOLLYWOOD AND VINES (Diagram 15 W)

This summit band extends 400 feet along the West Bluff Trail and is named for two towers below a recessed section at the northern part of the wall. The east, vine-covered tower is Hollywood; the other tower is Vines. The harder route on each is on the east side. Broken summit rocks continue north for another 150 feet. The region is directly above the north shore of the lake.

ACCESS: Follow the West Bluff Trail 850 feet south from its northern terminus to an access at the south end of the rock band.

1   5.7–5.9. Several variations are possible on this short face, which is harder on the left (south) side.

2   5.6. V-chimney with a wide crack on southeast side of south buttress. Climb on left side of the V or in right crack, first as a chimney, then on the outside when the crack narrows and finally splits.

3   5.7. Start just left of corner and climb straight to top.
    *Variation,* 5.8. Same start, but finish in layback crack on the right (north) side.

4   NEVER AGAIN, 5.8–5.9, depending on fist size. Climb blocks leading to a wider crack, jam your way up the crack (requires a good-sized fist).

5   5.10b. Climb lower and upper smooth face directly from the bottom.
    *Variation,* 5.8. Start up on the north side, traverse around east corner to ledge, finish on a smooth upper face.

6   5.10a. Climb, staying on north side of corner to top.

7   5.7. There is a large oak tree growing at an unnatural angle across the wall, blocking the start of this climb, as well as a couple of potential routes. Start climb by walking up the trunk 4 feet.

8   5.6. Climb wall with three large flakes, following the flakes.

9   5.8. Climb corner accentuated by a reddish rib or prominence to overhanging crack that, luckily, contains a chockstone (albeit a loose one).

10  5.8. Climb the corner, using a projecting rock finger for a

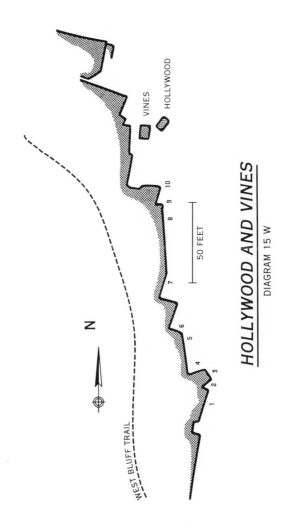

N

WEST BLUFF TRAIL

VINES

HOLLYWOOD

50 FEET

*HOLLYWOOD AND VINES*

DIAGRAM 15 W

foothold, then climb the overhang directly or follow the overhanging crack to top.

THE BOTTOM is a hidden spot below the branch trail that runs parallel to the base of Hollywood and Vines. Where this trail draws even with the south end of Hollywood and Vines, a short ridge extends downward (east) about 100 feet, terminating abruptly in a wall 30 feet high and 40 feet wide. The wall has several climbs.

5.10a. Face and overhang 4 feet left of Left Cheek.

LEFT CHEEK, 5.8. South half of the wall. Climb slight rib with a small overhang near top.

THE HEART, 5.10a. Face route 4 to 5 feet right of Left Cheek.

5.4. Central crack. Climb crack, step right to a small pine tree to finish.

RIGHT CHEEK, 5.9. North half of the wall. This is a fuzzy route on down-sloping ledges.

## NORTH SLOPE (No Diagram)

The North Slope is the last rock band along the West Bluff Trail, 375 feet from the north terminus of the trail. The elevation of the bluff as you proceed north decreases rather rapidly. The trail follows some slabs along the edge of the bluff. The band is described from north to south.

BUTTRESS I

5.4. At northern end of the North Slope. Climb the north side of the buttress.

5.8. Climb southeast face and crack without use of left corner.

BUTTRESS II

5.5–5.7. Southeast side has nice face climbs.

BUTTRESS III

5.7. Climb the corner, starting as a layback on northeast

side. Buttress III is less pronounced than II or IV.
5.2. Access chimney on south side of Buttress III.

BUTTRESS IV
5.7. Overhanging ledges at the northeast corner.
5.5. Crack on the southeast side, 8 feet left of corner.
5.7. Face right of crack.
5.8. Face left of crack.

There are rocks continuing 50 feet to the south at a slightly lower level.

The first (north) section is a wall with mostly bucket holds, though it has a difficult start at the lowest point.

To the south (past a wide crack and an inside corner) there is a smooth narrow wall with vertical joints, which has an attractive face/crack climb (5.8).
The south side of this wall is a flake climb.

The rocks farther south offer little interest to climbers.

# The South Bluff

One of the most rewarding features at the South Bluff is the superb view of the lake and the East and West Bluffs. It is rarely visited by climbers. At one time there was a South Bluff Trail.

There is one outcropping consisting of several small towers located in the boulderfield near the top of the bluff. The three main towers can be seen from the south shore picnic area, across the valley from Leaning Tower. The 20 or more short climbs (5.2–5.10) should not be overlooked, as they offer a full day of climbing.

Below these towers at the base of the bluff is an old quarry cut which contains natural springs. Sometimes in the winter the springs build short ice walls useful for ice-climbing practice. The springs dry up after a succession of dry summers, but recover after a summer of normal rainfall.

Inasmuch as the South Bluff is not frequently visited, the likelihood of encountering a rattlesnake should not be overlooked.

# Bibliography

Armstrong, Patricia. 1966. "Devil's Lake, Geological Showplace of the Midwest," *Earth Science* (May–June), pp. 112–115.

Armstrong, Patricia K. S. 1968. Cryptogram Communities on Quartzite of Devil's Lake, Wisconsin. M.S. Thesis, University of Chicago.

Attig, John W., Lee Clayton, Kenneth I. Lange, and Louis J. Maher, 1990. *The Ice Age Geology of Devil's Lake State Park*. Madison: Geological and Natural History Survey. Education Series 35.

Black, Robert F. 1964. "Potholes and Associated Gravel of Devil's Lake State Park." *Wisconsin Academy of Sciences, Arts and Letters* 53: 165–175.

Black, Robert F. 1965. "Ice-wedge Casts of Wisconsin." *Wisconsin Academy of Sciences, Arts and Letters* 54: 187–222.

Black, Robert F. 1967–68. "Geomorphology of Devil's Lake Area, Wisconsin." *Wisconsin Academy of Sciences, Arts and Letters* 56: 117–148.

Curtis, John T. 1959. *The Vegetation of Wisconsin*. Madison: The University of Wisconsin Press.

Dalziel, I. W. D., R. H. Dott, Jr., R. F. Black, and J. H. Zimmerman. 1970. *Geology of the Baraboo District, Wisconsin*. Madison: Geological and Natural History Survey Information Circular no. 14.

Fassett, Norman C. 1931. *Spring Flora of Wisconsin*. Madison: The University of Wisconsin Press.

Fralick, Jack. 1941. Rock Climbing in the Chicago Area: An Historical Guide. Chicago. Unpublished manuscript, 90 pp.

Grayson, Don. 1992. *Mountaineering: The Freedom of the Hills*. 5th ed. Seattle: The Mountaineers.

Hermacinski, Leo. 1985. *Extremist's Guide to Devil's Lake New Climbs*. Privately printed.

Hermacinski, Leo. 1992. Extremist's Guide to Devil's Lake New Climbs (updated). Unpublished manuscript, 21 pp.

Lange, Kenneth I. 1989. *Ancient Rocks and Vanished Glaciers: A Natural History of Devil's Lake State Park, Wisconsin*. Stevens Point, WI: Worzalla Publishing Co.

Lange, Kenneth I., and Ralph T. Tuttle. 1975. *A Lake Where Spirits Live: A Human History of the Midwest's Most Popular Park*. Baraboo, WI: Baraboo Printing.

Plumley, William J. 1941. Rock Climbing in the Chicago Area. Chicago: Unpublished Manuscript, 55 pp.

Primak, William. 1965. *Guidebook to the Local Practice Climbing Areas of the Chicago Mountaineering Club, Devil's Lake Section.* Chicago: Chicago Mountaineering Club.

Smith, David, and Roger Zimmerman. 1970. *Climbers and Hikers Guide to Devil's Lake.* Madison: Wisconsin Hoofers.

# Index of Climbs and Areas